Why read thi

A wonderful book! Many of us are struggling to maintain hope in these times, as our problems loom larger and our solutions seem shrunken. In *Reason to Hope*, David Osborne inspires readers to explore a hope that is deeper than mere optimism, so we can live positively – even in the presence of so much negativity. The book is beautifully written, and great for group study.

Brian D. McLaren
Author of *Life After Doom* and *Faith After Doubt*

Facing an ecological crisis that he recognises as 'an enormous and multi-faceted problem', Osborne sets out to find if there is a reasonable basis for hope. From atoms to galaxies, from Genesis to Revelation, Osborne then takes us on an impressively researched and referenced romp through science and Christian theology in his search for the evidence. His search is articulate, scholarly in detail, while accessible to anyone on a similar journey.

Katharine M. Preston
Anthropologist, ecologist and theologian, New York State. Author of *Field with a View*.

How do we live our Hope in troubling times? What is the catalyst that transforms shared beliefs, values and norms into living Faith? Based on deep personal encounters with literature and life, David Osborne guides us on an empowering, enlightening, incarnational pilgrimage through the sacred landscapes of the natural sciences, social sciences, praise scripture and wisdom traditions to root our hope in a deeper understanding of the meaning, energy and *being* of God's incarnate love for the Whole of Creation. Whether used as a study guide or as a daily meditation, *Reason to Hope* will be your *anam cara* (soul friend) as you find abundant joy in the Mystery of Living Hope.

Richard A. Nisbett
Anthropologist, ecologist, and environmental activist, Alabama

Weighty topics … but written in a very accessible and winsome way, imbued with David's own deep and reflective faith.

Brett Nicholls
Accountant working with charities, Glasgow

Reason to Hope

Modern science, ancient wisdom and the ecological crisis

David Osborne

wild goose publications

www.ionabooks.com

First published 2025 by
Wild Goose Publications
Suite 9, Fairfield
1048 Govan Road, Glasgow G51 4XS, Scotland
A division of Iona Community Trading CIC
Limited Company Reg. No. SC156678
www.ionabooks.com

ISBN 978-1-80432-383-0

The publishers gratefully acknowledge the support of the Drummond Trust, 3 Pitt Terrace, Stirling FK8 2EY in producing this book.

Overseas distribution
Australia: Willow Connection Pty Ltd, 1/13 Kell Mather Drive, Lennox Head NSW 2478
New Zealand: Pleroma, Higginson Street, Otane 4170, Central Hawkes Bay

Printed in the UK by Page Bros (Norwich) Ltd

FSC www.fsc.org
MIX
Paper | Supporting responsible forestry
FSC® C023114

Contents

Introduction

Forty years ago, at Scargill House in Yorkshire, I came across what was called a 'Celtic blessing':

> Deep peace of the running wave to you.
> Deep peace of the flowing air to you.
> Deep peace of the quiet earth to you.
> Deep peace of the shining stars to you.
> Deep peace of the Son of Peace to you.

It was attributed to the Iona Community and sparked my interest. I found out more and after a while I joined the Community.

That short prayer became for me a kind of mantra, or a framework for meditation. At times I would sit in a favourite place, below a particular oak tree in a field above my house, or watching the sea, or at home in my study, and recite the prayer slowly, giving myself time to visualise each phrase. Waves rolling into a shore. The wind blowing through long grass. The rich soil below the trees and grass. Or the stars on a clear night.

Sometimes I would make up other verses about a flowing stream, or the shining sun, flying birds, or drifting clouds. It gave me a sense of connection, and of an underlying peace in the world I was part of. But then it stopped.

When I imagined waves I thought of plastic litter washed up on beaches, accumulating in oceans, choking turtles and entering the vital organs of fish. When I thought of flowing air I thought of the atmosphere gradually warming, and the storms and torrential rains that come with it. The quiet earth was being stripped of its fertility by pesticides, soil loss, and pollution. The shining stars were cold, passive and unimaginably distant. And I was not sure how peaceful the so-called Son of Peace actually was.

My concern about the ecological crisis was that so little was being done to address what is an enormous and multifaceted problem. I had been conscious of many aspects of the problem for fifty years and involved with others in many activities to try to produce change locally, in the church, and in society as a whole. Many of the things we argued or campaigned for are at last beginning to happen but it feels like too little too late.

It is encouraging that the BBC and other media channels now treat climate change not as a theory but as a fact that needs urgent attention. We see more waste being recycled and more energy conserved or created from renewable sources. Attitudes in agriculture are changing and organic production is becoming more mainstream. Tree planting is encouraged and more areas are preserved for wildlife. But it is so little in the face of what is happening to life on earth.

We are, of course, not the first generation that has faced a great crisis, and knowing that can be a comfort. People in the past have also had deep-seated fears for the future. There have been disasters such as the Black Death, the First World War and the Cold War, all of which humanity survived, albeit at a tremendous cost. But just because we survived those does not mean we will survive the next.

My own gloom was compounded by other people's. I belong to communities and networks in which many people share a concern about what is happening to the earth. Some are very active political campaigners. Others work on local projects to improve their environment. Some try to influence their employers to develop greener ways of operating. They all try to adjust their way of living to make their carbon footprint smaller, and to reduce their single- use plastics and other pollutants. And they try to remain positive. But it is hard when there is so much bad news.

Many of us have things we can do which we know may well pick up our mood if we are sad or depressed about something. These activities do not solve the problem, but they help us feel hopeful. Being out in nature was a favourite with many people during the Covid lockdowns. Talking with friends, listening to or making music, reading novels, doing puzzles, cooking, making things: these are all helpful, and sometimes they can be lifesavers. They can stop us spiralling down into a mood where we cannot summon the will or the energy to do anything.

But the problem is still there and while doing these things might make us feel more hopeful, we can also have a lurking suspicion that whatever hope we feel has no real basis: that it is simply a passing emotion.

I wanted to tackle the question of whether there is any reasonable basis for hope. Can hope be more than a feeling triggered by our activities or circumstances? I set out to address this question and this book is the outcome. My answer is set out in five stages.

The first stage teases out what we mean by hope, and how it differs from optimism. We then go on to think about what the world is like. I do not go to great lengths describing the nature of the ecological crisis we face as that is done in so many other books as well as articles, podcasts and TV programmes. But I sketch out several of the ways we make sense of the world we are part of. This leads on to us looking at one particular historic response to the sense many people have that there is more to the world than simply matter: the Hebrew and Christian scriptures. We then see whether we can interpret what they say from their ancient culture into our own understanding of the world and society. And this finally leads us to an answer to the question, and one which leaves the door open to looking for further encouragement and hope in other places.

Covering such a lot of ground in so few words inevitably means that what is here is like a painting with a broad brush, or a sketch. To follow what I am saying you do not need to know anything to begin with about, say, modern physics, psychology, religious studies, or theology. If you do you may well find what I say here insufficiently nuanced or detailed, but the alternative was either to produce a much longer, and therefore possibly indigestible, book, or ignore what are very relevant fields of study and important parts of the argument.

However, there are plenty of notes which you can use if you want to check out my sources or find out more about what I am saying. They include references to some of the books and websites I have drawn on, possible sources of further information, and sometimes a little more about a subject.

At the end of the book there is a list of recommended reading which you may find helpful if you want to find out more about a subject which I have considered very briefly. The list gives authors, titles and enough information to track a book down, and also some brief information about each book which might help you decide whether or not to go for it. But first, we need to clarify what it is we are thinking about.

Part 1

OPENING THE QUESTION

Chapter 1
Optimism, hope and reason

Four children and a dog were having an adventure in the Highlands.

'We'll be fine,' said Justin. 'And the view will be superb.'

Anna was concerned that they did not have proper equipment for climbing a mountain. It was a sunny day but there were clouds on some of the tops.

'It's only Scotland,' said Justin. 'It's not the Himalayas.'

So they carried on up the path towards the summit. The cloud got thicker, and Anna suggested that they turn back.

'It'll clear when we get to the top,' said Georgia. 'Imagine what it'll be like to have the clouds open and to be able to see for miles.'

'And anyway,' she added, 'we've got Tommy to look after us.'

'We can have our lunch when we get there,' said Dick. 'Salmon sandwiches and Dundee cake.'

But the cloud thickened and it became harder to see the path. What had been a drizzle turned into rain.

The five turned round when they thought they were at the top but the downward path was hard to see. Anna was clearly worried. Their trainers were beginning to slip on the wet rock and grass. Justin went on ahead.

'I can see where the path goes,' he said. 'Don't worry. We'll be fine.'

Then Georgia, Anna and Dick heard sliding stones, and a shout from Justin that cut off suddenly. The sound of stones falling went on for a long time. Tommy began to bark but there was no answer when they called Justin.

At that point Anna got out her mobile phone and called the emergency services. Mountain Rescue found the three children after a couple of hours, helped by Tommy's barking. They were wet through and suffering from hypothermia.

They recovered Justin's body as it began to get dark. Unless Justin had meant something very unusual by 'We'll be fine', he was wrong.

It is a common scenario for Mountain Rescue teams: finding people who have gone up without proper clothing, and then failed to turn back when the weather deteriorated. Lifeboat crews find people who have set out to cross the sea in inadequate boats. Fire and Rescue teams cut out the bodies of people who have set out in their car having drunk too much but been quite confident they can drive safely, while ambulance crews deal with the people their cars have hit. Teachers have to try to get through to enthusiastic parents that their musical child is quite good but is not a new Mozart. Counsellors hear from people about how their marriage, despite all their hopes at the beginning and efforts since then, has fallen apart.

These people had felt hopeful when they set off on foot or in their boat or car, when they heard their child playing the violin, or when they made vows in a marriage ceremony. Things would work out well. Things would be good. But they were mistaken and their hopes were dashed by reality. It is all very well feeling hopeful but that feeling can be misplaced. There are numerous people who when they were young were optimistic about becoming a professional footballer, or a singer, or a model, but it never happened. It must be a rare person who has not suffered a major disappointment at some time in their life.

Looking for hope

Before the COP26 conference in Glasgow, Kathy Galloway, an environmental campaigner and former Leader of the Iona Community, was asked if she was optimistic. She said, 'No, but I am hopeful.' It is probably helpful to distinguish between optimism and hope.

Optimism can be hard work. To be optimistic we have to keep looking for the good things that are happening. But the news we hear is so often bad that we have to look through it, or look elsewhere, or try to find a silver lining in a very dark cloud. And sometimes, something that seemed good can turn out to have serious downsides. Or a person who seemed reliable can in time prove inadequate. Or people who should work together bicker and fall out. The optimist has to see the glass as half full, not half empty, and that is hard when the glass only has a few drops in the bottom, or it is cracked.

But hope is something else: something deeper. In *Strictly Come Dancing* the judges are looking for someone who can dance well, but they are also looking for flair. And it could be that the person who has that additional factor is not technically the best dancer. On another channel is the *BBC Young Musician* competition. To win that someone has to be technically very good but the judges are also looking for something deeper: a musicality which enables them not only to play well but to interpret the music with sensitivity, imagination, and their own creativity.

Hope is like that. It is deeper than optimism. It is more secure. It does not need to be continually fed with positive information. It is perhaps like joy in comparison with humour. Or like peace in comparison with contentment. If we are looking for hope we are not necessarily looking for more positive information about the world but a way to live positively in it.

Optimism requires a stream of reasons for being positive whereas hope involves facing what is going wrong and seeing beyond it. That is going to mean having a big picture. Or, to put it another way, hope involves having a deep sense that somehow we will get through the bad even if it is not possible in the present circumstances to see how that might happen.

This suggests that a basis for hope is not going to be simply a list of reasons to be positive about the future based on current evidence. It is going to be bigger or deeper than that. But it also, somehow, has to relate to the world as it actually is or it is worthless. Harsh reality will get the better of a pleasant fantasy. We need a basis for hope which can face up to our knowledge of what is happening in the world and fits with the understanding of the world that we have through science and history.

Dangers in the dark

Being pursued by a malignant force is a familiar theme of dreams and stories. In a dream the solution is to turn, if we can, and to face the pursuer: to look and see what it actually is. In the same way, counsellors sometimes find that when someone is anxious or fearful it is helpful to explore what it is that they are actually afraid of: what is happening in their life that is generating the fear. So, in order to work out whether there is a reasonable basis for hope in the situation that we find ourselves in we need to look at that situation, and particularly at what it is that challenges our hopefulness.

One danger in doing this is that it is possible to lose sight of what is good about the society and world we are part of. There is music and laughter, great art, and people caring about each other. There are people who give up successful careers to work in refugee camps or to campaign on a particular issue for the good of other people. There are thousands of grassroots movements across the world working for social and environmental justice, and sometimes attitudes, laws and policies change as a result of such action.

We can see how people working together can achieve a great deal. The Covid vaccination programme is just one example of what international co-operation in science is able to do. Co-operation between nation states has brought the blue whale back from the edge of extinction, banned CFCs, and brought war criminals to justice. There are moves now to designate ecocide as a crime. And there are still beautiful sunsets and sometimes birdsong at dawn. There is much that is good, but it can disappear from view when we are thinking about what is going wrong. We may be unable to recognise these things or, if we know they are there, to enjoy them.

If we are able to appreciate life, that can make the slow pace of change particularly frustrating and hearing bad news even more painful. If we appreciate our local patch of woodland, we will feel strongly about a proposal to clear it for a bypass. If we enjoy the dawn chorus, an article about the decline in songbirds will make us feel more disappointed. If we live in a place with a strong sense of community, we can feel anxious about the area being radically altered. If we enjoy life and have ideas for the future, we will feel sad about it possibly ending soon.

In order to think about hope we need to face up to the issues which can challenge our hopefulness, and at the same time try not to lose sight of what is good in the world. Somehow, we need a balance. If we get too low we lack the energy or drive to do anything. But if we avoid all thought of the problems we face, we do not address them.

Anger and action

Fear and anger can motivate us to take action and sometimes we can do something to address and try to solve problems. We can campaign for action on climate change and adapt our lifestyle. We can become involved with a political party or pressure group. We can do things to help friends in difficulties or to improve our own health. Doing something, however small, helps us feel more hopeful. We are then no longer victims but actors, and we are making a difference.

All this is good. It is essential. Problems rarely solve themselves. To address the climate crisis, we need to take action to adjust our way of living and to pressurise those in power to make necessary changes. To reduce plastic pollution, we need to cut down on our own use of non-biodegradable plastics. Feeding hungry people, housing the homeless, bringing honesty into political debate, removing weapons of mass destruction, creating justice for marginalised or mistreated people, resolving local or global conflicts: all these require action. Often, we cannot take action ourselves but we can still support and encourage those who can. We feel better for being involved in the struggles.

It is perhaps inevitable that action makes us feel better. If way back in the mists of time our human predecessors had not felt compelled to solve their problems, and felt better in doing so, humans would not have survived. It is instinctive. Animals, birds, and insects all take evasive action when they sense danger. The drive to continue despite great challenges must be very deep in our brain structure. It must be hardwired into us to have a sense of hope, even against enormous odds. We have needed it to survive so far.[1]

But the question remains, and sometimes it surfaces. We can take action for change, and we can do things that will make us feel more hopeful, but does this hope have any reasonable basis? The question can surface when we are tired, or restricted in what we are able to do. It can surface when we have been trying hard to produce a change but seem to be getting nowhere, or when another piece of bad news rolls in. Or it can suddenly surface in our minds for no apparent reason: when we are sitting on a bus, or washing dishes, or when we wake up in the middle of the night. Is there really any hope?

Dreams and distractions

Of course, hope will mean different things for different people. Mountaineers hope to reach their destination and return without injury. Sailors, for good weather and a safe voyage. Motorists, for no breakdowns or accidents and light traffic. Someone facing an operation, for better health afterwards. A couple attending counselling, for a better relationship. And so on.

In the face of big crises such as climate change, pollution, arms proliferation, increasing poverty, and war, our hopes are probably more diffuse and more precarious. It is easy to tick off the marks of a successful mountaineering or sailing trip, and to measure when or whether there has been an improvement in our health. People in a relationship might well be able to look back and say that they have passed through a rough patch. Bigger issues are harder to assess as they have many facets and might be very long term. For example, the way the earth's climate is changing is affecting different regions in different ways. Any reduction in the rate of change will register in global statistics but mean very different things in different places. Or there could be a limitation on the production of nuclear weapons, or even a global agreement for their eradication, but chemical and biological weapons might still be produced. So, in these cases, while short- or medium-term goals can be established and possibly achieved, the ultimate hope is less clear.

In the sixties Ed McCurdy wrote a song in which he had a dream that the world had agreed to put an end to war. The picture was of men in a room signing a document while outside people were dancing all around, with guns and swords and uniforms lying on the ground.[2] It is a beautiful picture but not a realistic aim for the outcome of an international agreement. Perhaps in the face of the really big issues we can only resort to dreams and visions for our ultimate hopes. They can be inspiring, encouraging and draw us forward, but they are never going to feature in the news as having been achieved.

The question is whether they have any reasonable basis or are just dreams. And perhaps if our wonderful visions are unrealistic they are dangerous, like the picture in Justin's imagination of arriving at the top of the mountain and enjoying the view while they ate their salmon sandwiches. Or they might be distractions. Songs and stories can inspire and energise but producing real change also involves people taking part in long and tedious negotiations, often in boring meetings with agendas and targets. Those too are necessary.

What we are looking for

If hope means different things to different people, and depends on what they are engaged in, perhaps it is not even meaningful to talk generally about 'hope' as something real. But we talk about 'music', although it only exists in the playing of instruments and in songs and performances. We talk about 'sport', although we only experience it in games, matches, challenges and competitions. A million poets have written about love but it only exists in people's relationships. And humour exists in particular jokes and comic situations. If we can think and talk about music, sport, love, and humour, as well as childhood, aging, creativity, and other things which we experience only in specific instances, we can also think about hope as something real, though it exists for us only in specific situations.

Whether we think of hope as a generality from our multitude of experiences or some sort of phenomenon which manifests itself in different ways is not the issue. And trying to settle that issue would take us on a philosophical diversion which we can leave aside for now.[3] The point is that if it makes sense to talk about music, sport, humour, and so on, it also makes sense to think and talk about hope. If we can work out generally what hope is, and find reasons for hope, we can then think how they might work out in different ways in particular situations. It may be that there is reason to hope in almost any situation. If there is, it would be good to find it. And even if our idea of hope is not absolutely clear at the moment we can assume we will recognise it when we see it.[4]

In order to root our thinking about hope in the reality of the present we need to look more closely at the nature of the crisis we are in. I am not going to go in detail through the litany of issues we face: climate change, pollution, species decline, population growth, water shortages, flooding, mass migration, war, pandemics, and so on. These are well known to anyone who cares to find out. The information is there on the websites of NGOs, in books, magazines, news reports, and even on the websites of some government departments. Anyone who does not know that there is a crisis, does not want to know, and is probably working hard to avoid the information or suppress the knowledge.

The mess we are in

We know that there is much that is wonderful in the world and it is important not to lose sight of that. As well as the beauty of the world we are part of, there are people who care about each other, and some remarkable human achievements. There is music, painting, poetry, engineering, antibiotics, computers … Billions of people now live with a standard of housing and diet which would have been the lifestyle of only a very few a couple of centuries ago. But there is also a mess, and it is this that makes us anxious and depressed.

The problems could be thought of as of three kinds. Many of them are the consequences of what seemed like a good idea at the time. The burning of coal, the production of concrete, the development of steam power, then the internal combustion engine all improved many people's lives. But now we have climate change as a consequence. In the 1950s plastics took off as the wonder material. Anyone who can remember wooden kitchen furniture, metal toys with sharp edges, and rubber electrical insulation is likely to feel that plastic improved life in many ways. But now plastic nanoparticles are in our watercourses and our bloodstreams. Antibiotics and other pharmaceuticals in the last fifty years have saved millions of lives, but they are now damaging our waterways, soil, many ecosystems, and so much more.

We could go on. The point is that many features of life in our Western society which were hailed as great advances have also, over time, had a downside. This is sometimes not because they are inherently dangerous but because they have been overused or misused. Or they were intended as a benefit to humanity and perhaps to other life as well but have become harmful in the long term.

But there are some things which are deliberately harmful to people or to other life. From bullying to warfare, from petty theft to tax evasion, from malicious gossip to fake news, from simple lies to published misinformation, people do things which might benefit them but will clearly harm other people. The harm is not an unfortunate consequence but an aim.

There are other things which just happen, or at least have no human agent. Dementia and cancer, earthquakes and volcanos, viral pandemics and bacterial diseases are all part of how the world is. Often people could do more to alleviate or avoid the problems these cause to other people or themselves, but people do not deliberately cause them.

All these contribute to the suffering of life on the planet, and to our anxiety and distress. It is in the context of all such things that we need hope. The mess we are in is not simply the result of people doing bad things; there is a lot more to it than that. And to find reason to hope we need to think more about the world we are part of.

Part 2

ANALYSIS

Chapter 2

One, weird and wonderful:
The world we are part of

David Attenborough started presenting programmes about wildlife on British television in the 1950s. Sixty years later he was still at it but by then the focus had changed. No longer was he on *Zoo Quest* in Borneo or Madagascar looking for rare animals, but now the programmes were about *Planet Earth*, about oceans, mountains, forests, rivers and even cities and industrial wastelands. We would still see the species but the focus was now on habitats and ecosystems, about how species interact with their environment and with each other, about the challenges that are presented to a species when that environment changes, and how a species can alter its environment.

The RSPB[1] was founded to protect birds threatened by hunting for the use of their feathers as fashion items. The organisation continues to protect birds, as the name says, but it now largely does it by protecting environments: marshes, estuaries, forests, moorlands, old quarries and peat cuttings, whatever kind of place it is that the birds need in order to thrive. People will go to an RSPB site to look at avocets, or bar-tailed godwits, or whatever, but the organisation's work is looking after the place for the birds. Giving a home to nature, as they say in their publicity.

The change of focus from individual species to environments moved significantly in the seventies with James Lovelock's insight into naturally occurring feedback systems on the planet.[2] Referring to this dynamic network as 'Gaia', his insight enabled people to think not just about individual animals, birds or insects, or about species, or specific environments, but also about the whole of life on the earth as if it was one living organism: one whole, of which we humans are a part.

The interaction of animals and their environments

Many animals alter their environment by making nests or burrowing holes. Beavers build dams to form pools to protect their lodges. But no species has altered its environment as dramatically as *Homo sapiens*, with our cities, roads, mines, factories, power stations, cars, planes and weapons. The present period of time has been dubbed the 'Anthropocene' epoch as the changes we have made are on a geological scale and are altering the earth's climate away from the fairly stable climatic systems of the Holocene epoch, which the planet has enjoyed for the last 12,000 years, to something much less predictable.

This is happening at great cost to other life forms. We are altering the landscape, oceans and atmosphere by our ways of living. Deserts are spreading, oceans are acidifying, the atmosphere is warming, and weather patterns are changing. As less rain falls in a dry area, fewer plants grow, and as less grows more of the water that does fall simply runs off, making it even harder for what plants remain to flourish. This kind of cycle spins a million times on the planet.

By our burning of fossil fuels since the Industrial Revolution we have released into the atmosphere a vast amount of carbon dioxide which had been stored millennia ago, and this is consequently changing the earth's climate. Over a hundred years ago it was shown in the laboratory that air with a higher carbon dioxide content allowed less heat to pass through it, and so would have an insulating effect on the earth.[3] But only in the nineteen seventies was 'the greenhouse effect' being widely acknowledged. Now we are seeing it in all parts of the world. In Britain we have hotter summers and heavier rain when it comes. In the sub-Arctic tundra the permafrost is melting. In the Arctic, the Antarctic and the high Alps, glaciers are melting at a faster rate than at any time in recorded history. In the tropics, deserts are spreading, and increased flooding is destroying agricultural land.

There is a sad irony in this. Part of the increase in demand for energy from fossil fuels has been driven by a continually rising demand for more and more consumer goods. A slogan of many environment campaigners is that we cannot have continual growth on a finite planet. The cause is good: we clearly do not all need more stuff. We cannot all have the same material standard of living as that enjoyed by the rich people of North America and Europe. The planet simply cannot provide the materials that would be needed or the human cost and environmental impact of more and more factories.

However, the planet is not a totally closed system. It has a finite amount of matter but every moment of every day it is receiving vast quantities of energy from the sun. A small amount of this is harnessed with solar panels, or indirectly in wind farms which take energy from the movement of air caused by temperature changes in the atmosphere. The technology exists to harness much more, in that it has been invented, but relatively little is being deployed. Much of the world's oil comes from countries that have more heat than they know what to do with but until now they have done little to harness it.[4] The gravitational attraction of the moon and sun causes tides in the earth's oceans, but little is being done to harness the energy of this continual movement of water, even in Britain which has significant tidal flows around its coasts.

Developing more solar and tidal power would contribute to a country's economic growth in the same way as would building more coal-fired power stations. The problem is not so much growth in itself, as the way that economic growth is pursued as if growth were always valuable, without asking what is actually growing, who is benefitting, and how sustainable particular aspects of economic activity are.[5]

Unfortunately, climate change is just one of a number of major problems that humanity has caused for life on the planet. We could go on and think about the removal of forests for food production and the consequent extinction of species, about overfishing, the possible consequences of seabed mining, about water shortages, and chemical and plastic pollution. But information about these and other threats is available in many places. The point is that we are one of a multitude of species which inhabit this planet and which are all interconnected, and by our actions we are causing harm to the whole ecosystem of this blue planet we call home.

So why is it that we are not doing more to limit or even rectify the damage we do? We will return to that question in the next chapter but in order to think about the wider question of hope, we also need to think about the nature of the world we are part of.

A different centre

Recognising connections between different species is not new. Hunter-gatherers knew where to look for particular foods. Nomadic pastoralists knew they had to take their cattle or sheep to particular environments. Traditional farmers knew a great deal about which crops to plant where and with which others. The science of ecology has refined and developed this knowledge and, following Darwin, there has been a recognition of how, in the long term, environments affect species while species also alter their environments. But in the study of physics there has been not so much a development within the last few centuries as a series of revolutions.

We still speak in English about a 'sunset' but we know the sun is not actually setting. It is the earth that is turning. This was one of the great revolutions in thinking that happened in the seventeenth century. Nicolaus Copernicus looked at the information astronomers had accumulated about the sun, moon, stars and planets, and saw it differently. His new pattern made more sense of the very odd movements of the so-called 'wandering stars', or planets. He reckoned the sun was at the centre and the planets went round them.

People were not convinced at first. Galileo Galilei was, but he was pressurised by a very angry Catholic Church to deny it. However, in time more measurements were taken, Johannes Kepler refined the theory, and it became accepted. A century later Isaac Newton came up with the theory of gravity to explain how it worked: how it is that the earth does not shoot off into space and why small objects such as apples fall to the ground.[6] Newton's Laws of Motion explain how it happens and provide what has been called the Classic Model of physics, which portrays the universe as in some ways like a great machine. The model expands into the laws put forward by Robert Boyle concerning pressure, volume and temperature, by James Clerk Maxwell and Georg Ohm concerning electricity, and a host of others working in the eighteenth and nineteenth centuries.

The relativity revolution

Watching a sunset we all know that it is really the earth turning but still feel we are watching the sun set. Relative to us, standing at one point on the earth, the sun is moving, and relativity was the idea that produced another scientific revolution in the early twentieth century. Albert Einstein imagined what the universe would be like if he was moving at the speed of light. The final outcome of his thinking, calculations and numerous discussions was the General Theory of Relativity. According to this almost everything is relative. The speed of light is a constant but space and time are so interrelated that scientists began to talk about 'spacetime'. Matter and energy are interchangeable, contrary to the formerly established Principle of Conservation of Energy.

In time, following numerous experiments, support for Einstein's theory grew. The 1945 atomic explosion turned matter into energy as he had predicted. It was then worked out how to make even bigger bombs using a fusion of hydrogen atoms, the process by which the sun generates the energy which radiates out into the universe, a tiny fraction of which washes over the earth. Other stars are similar, and in the course of their 'life' they make hydrogen into helium, carbon and other elements. These elements might form gas clouds in space. Some combine to form minerals which come together to form solid bodies such as asteroids and planets.

This formation has been a long process and it is set to continue for a long time yet as the universe expands. It is now reckoned that the universe began with a singular event 13.8 billion years ago, dubbed 'the Big Bang', and that within this universe are not only solid bodies and clouds but also dark matter, which is invisible, and vast amounts of dark energy which influences how light and matter move within the universe. Einstein worked out that gravity attracts not only matter but also light and it was then discovered that there are in the universe black holes which have such massive density that light cannot escape from them.

Einstein also predicted that time would change in relation to velocity and mass, as time was also relative. That too has been proven to be true. A very sensitive timepiece moved around the world in a fast jet moves out of sync with one which is kept in the same place. And time moves more slowly at the top of a mountain than it does down in a valley. So it is reckoned that at the edge of a black hole time comes to a halt, which raises fascinating questions. We generally assume that time goes on a steady rate, even when it does not feel like that to us, but how real is time? Does it go in a line or round in a circle?[7]

The small picture

At the same time as science has been exploring the universe on the big scale, in the last two centuries there have been enormous developments in understanding the universe on the small scale. It was discovered that not only is matter made of atoms bonded into molecules, but that atoms are not the smallest component. The atoms are made up not only of protons, electrons and neutrons, but of a large number of smaller particles, and that under some circumstances some particles behave like waves.

Contrary to appearances, solid matter is largely space occupied by minute particles, bonded by various forces. We do not see it as such. We see and feel it as solid because we have what has been called 'blurred vision'. It is like looking at a bowl of sugar across a large room: we see it as a white mass, not as a pile of sugar grains. It is like looking at a window with a net curtain from a long distance: the window simply appears grey. On our scale, metal, stone, glass and plastic are solid.

On the subatomic scale, strange things happen with matter and energy. Energy, it seems, needs to be thought of as consisting in discrete units, which are called 'quanta', and exploring the behaviour of quanta is a whole field of scientific theory and debate. It seems that long after quanta have collided with each other they maintain some kind of relationship; so they exist in a myriad of interactions and interconnections.[8]

Random behaviour

Also, the behaviour of subatomic particles appears to be random. Uranium isotopes decay at a steady rate on the medium scale but if one particular atom is observed it cannot be predicted when it will suddenly change. So, is the cosmos at this smallest of all scales fundamentally random? The random behaviour averages out on the larger scale, so matter remains predictable, but the average does not describe the detail.

This apparently random behaviour has opened up another whole field of science and mathematics, known as indeterminacy or Chaos theory, which relates not only to atomic particles but also to human behaviour, traffic flow, fluid mechanics and weather forecasting. It seems that while something may appear random, at another level there may be a pattern. The numbers that describe the behaviour of traffic, say, may be a random sequence, but there may be a pattern in the degree of randomness, or at another higher level of analysis.[9]

It has long been known that obviously random behaviour can be triggered by a small event. For example, water running through a weir can be flowing smoothly even as the amount of water increases but it can suddenly be turned into 'white water' by one very small increase in flow or a disturbance. The mathematics of Chaos describes this.

A small change in one part of a system can produce significant changes elsewhere. The classic example of this is the so-called 'butterfly effect' in which, as it was put in a scientific paper presenting the idea in 1972, a butterfly flapping its wings in the Amazon jungle produces a tornado in Texas.[10] This presents problems for weather forecasters. Not that butterflies are a great threat but there are many other factors which can influence the interplay of air flow, humidity, pressure and temperature, which are the constituent parts of a weather system. Reliable weather forecasting beyond a few days has proved to be very difficult.

The difficulty lies in having enough information to begin with. If it is the case that seemingly random behaviour is actually, at some level, following a pattern, and if that pattern can be identified, it should be possible to predict what will happen. But, as small changes can produce big effects, forecasters need to know everything that might be relevant, and they cannot do that.

This raises an interesting logical issue about prediction. There is not just one butterfly flying around in the Amazon jungle. There are millions more between there and Texas, and they are all flapping their wings. The air they each move interacts with that moved by the others, as well as by the birds, planes, bats, footballs, and other objects which also disturb the air. There is an enormous network of interactions, so to predict something with total accuracy we would need to know absolutely everything that might influence the outcome, which is impossible.

In the mix

The science of the big scale and the science of the small scale are connected and the interplay of predictability and randomness, of necessity and chance, is seen at all levels of the cosmos. Here on our planet we see it in the behaviour of groups of people and animals. It means that such things as economic activity, crowd and traffic movements, and fashion trends have elements that can be foreseen, but are also full of surprises.

It is noticeable in the migrations and movements of animals. On the Somerset Levels in the evening vast flocks of starlings gather in a murmuration before roosting for the night. The movement of these flocks has a regularity about it, in that the birds are not moving in all directions, but the movement cannot be predicted. For days the birds might roost at Shapwick Heath, and then one evening when birders have gathered there to see the spectacle, the birds go to Ham Wall instead.

At a smaller scale, the mutation of genes happens randomly, although normally there is enough regularity for a cell or body to survive. Every starling in a flock is unique, although it has much in common with every other bird of the same species. It is mutations that give rise to individual characters amid family likenesses, which we are familiar with among humans. Mutation and natural selection mean that over time the starlings in one part of the world might differ significantly from those in another.

Mathematical wonders

Chaos theory is just one field of mathematics where the tools developed for one study can be used in a very different one. Mathematical methods, designs for equipment, and theoretical models can often be applied elsewhere. The principle is that what is true in one place will be true in another if the conditions are identical. This means that an idea like Chaos theory and its associated mathematical procedures can be applied to subatomic particles, water flowing through pipes or swirling around in tanks, global weather systems and the movement of asteroids, gas clouds and nebulae. Despite the vast differences of scale, it is one universe.

Recent work in cosmology has identified a number of significant forces that are at work throughout the cosmos from the subatomic to the stellar scale. A remarkable feature of these forces is how significantly different the universe would be if they were just very slightly different. If the electrical forces that hold atoms together were only a fraction of a percentage less, there would be a tiny universe, animals could grow no bigger than insects and there would be no time for biological evolution. If the amount of matter in the universe were larger it would have collapsed long ago, and if it had been too low no stars or galaxies would have been formed. If cosmic 'antigravity' were any larger it would have stopped galaxies and stars from forming, so the universe would not even have got started. If there were anything other than three spatial dimensions, life would not exist.[11]

The Classic Model of the universe is gone. We are part of an expanding universe with millions of galaxies, gas clouds, supernovae and black holes. All matter seems to be composed of the atoms of ninety-two elements, made within the stars. There is also antigravity, dark matter, dark energy and other forces operating at the cosmic and subatomic levels. There is predictable activity and also what appears random: everything is much more complex, dynamic and interconnected than the Classic Model suggested. We are not in a nursery rhyme, we are part of a great symphony. We are not splashing around in a paddling pool but swimming in a vast ocean. The cosmos is not like a clock but more like an organism. And we are a part of the whole.

Chapter 3

Trying to make sense of people: Ten perspectives

In the face of what is happening to life on earth we inevitably ask why more is not being done. There are interminable discussions and meetings but not enough happens. Targets are sometimes agreed, but then watered down. Meanwhile, many people and organisations carry on as if everything is fine: business as usual. This can drive us from frustration towards despair precisely because it is people who are causing the problems and people who are failing to address them. When I first had a cancer diagnosis I was upset, fearful, and sad at the thought that my life might end sooner than I would wish. But the cancer is impersonal. Being threatened by another person adds another dimension. They should not be doing this. Cancers, meteorites, volcanos and earthquakes are impersonal, but people make decisions about what they do. And the ecological crisis we are in is being caused by people.

Humans have tried to understand the behaviour of other people for a very long time; probably for as long as they have tried to understand anything. Many of us even find ourselves something of a puzzle at times. Over the centuries numerous explanations of human behaviour have developed. In some of these it is seen as influenced by external forces: planets and stars, or demons, spirits, angels and gods. Or a person is seen as being influenced by someone else in an unseen way, through magic or prayer. In other explanations it is internal forces that are at work: humours or energies which need to be balanced. We will briefly consider ten explanations of human behaviour which have been prevalent for the last century or so, particularly with regard to people who have, or claim to have, significant power.

1. People are people

The first thing to do is to remind ourselves of the obvious, that people are people. It needs saying, partly because those with power and influence can easily forget that those with little or nothing are like them. And those who have little can feel that those with wealth and power are something different from them. People who live on the seventh floor of a high-rise with a broken lift and urine in the stairwell are not a different kind of being from those who live in a mews in Chelsea or a mansion in Chalfont St Giles. But those with little can easily feel that the social elite are some kind of superbeing.

Emperors and kings have played on this. With their fancy clothes, large retinues, palaces and mansions, the powerful have intimidated the poor. Britain still has its monarchy and there are many people who do not want their royals downsized to what they disparagingly refer to as a 'Scandinavian-style' royal family. However, TV and social media now provide much of the aura that the trappings of wealth and power used to play. People will feel shy in the presence of someone they have seen frequently on TV. But they are all people: no more, and no less.

2. *Nature and nurture*

How a child develops is a consequence of both their physical, genetic, makeup and the influences upon them. There is a long running debate about the extent to which someone's personality is the result of nature or nurture, but it is surely both. In the same way that genetic makeup can influence a person's appearance or shape, so too can it influence their skills and aptitudes, as can their environment: parents, schooling, home opportunities, the availability of safe green space, etc.

If a growing child's social environment is unhealthy it might be called 'damaging'. Parental drug abuse, violence or neglect will have a profound effect on a growing child, and damage can be passed from generation to generation. Violence can breed violence. Bullies tend to create bullies. It is not inevitable and cycles can be, and often are, broken. But the evidence is that disorders such as psychopathy are often partly the result of the person's experience as a child.[1]

In some respects we are all damaged, including those who want political or economic power. Someone might have a number of motives for wanting power. They might want to change things for the good, or use it as an opportunity to benefit their own or their friends' bank accounts. They might have an unconscious need for recognition or achievement or a deep-seated fear of being insignificant.

3. There is more to us all than meets the eye

Like an iceberg, which is largely submerged, a large part of what makes us the people we are is below the surface. Freud and others explored the deep forces within the human psyche and numerous schools of psychological thought have developed. In some psychotherapy it is thought helpful to unearth the hidden fears and fantasies of the unwell person, on the basis that once they understand better what is going on they will be able to manage it. Others, however, say this is unnecessary and that such practices as gestalt therapy, transactional analysis, and cognitive behavioural therapy are more effective, as they focus on what is happening in present relationships between people and the world. Neuroscience has shown how the human brain is layered, with a reptilian core, and when under serious threat people tend to revert to core unconscious reactions, such as the fight/flight response.

What we see is often not what we get. People can present themselves on social media or TV as having a particular personality but this may not be their true character. It may simply be a way of acting that works for them, which is good for votes or for future contracts. People close to them may be aware of other aspects of their character and see something more of the person behind the persona.

Sigmund Freud's one-time colleague, Carl Gustav Jung, thought in terms of people each having a shadow: an aspect of themselves which they kept hidden and were often unaware of but which influenced their behaviour. For Roberto Assagioli each person had not simply a shadow but a number of sub-personalities which each needed to be identified and acknowledged for the individual to grow into better psychological health. Like Freud, both Jung and Assagioli believed there was much of each person which was hidden but influential. They also believed there was an innate drive towards integration and wholeness.

In the 1930s American theologian and political philosopher Reinhold Niebuhr argued that much human injustice stems from a tension within each person between the ability to understand or imagine possible futures and an inability to bring them about. For example, we might imagine something bad happening to us which we cannot stop but think that if we had more money, or more power, then perhaps we could. As a result, people will often struggle for more and defend their positions of power and their resources. For some people, even enormous wealth or extreme power and influence are not enough. They are still driven by a deep fear and can never feel safe enough.[2]

This also plays out among those of more modest but still high income. For example, in some European and North American cities there is a large and increasing number of SUVs on the roads. These vehicles are ostensibly designed for rough country and can cope with snow, floods and steep inclines, which are rarely issues on city streets, but being bigger and stronger than lesser cars the drivers feel safer. They also create more carbon dioxide, which affects everybody.

Niebuhr strongly criticised some of the campaigns for social justice in his day, including the so-called Social Gospel movement, for being naive about power. He reckoned they underestimated the extent to which those who had power would use it to maintain injustices and to protect their position, because the powerful were driven by a very deep, sometimes unconscious, fear.

4. The child we were does not go away

Perhaps because we have all once been small weak children who needed someone to look after us, many adults continue to feel like this at times. However much 'tough' people may resist it, this is actually healthy. We sometimes need to regress into a state of dependence. A person who is seriously unwell needs to be able to allow their carer or doctor to do their work. People in caring professions need sometimes to stop caring for others and let someone look after them so they can recover perspective, energy, and a sense of themselves.

People in search of power will sometimes recognise that many other people want someone who will look after them and will unconsciously or deliberately use that. They might make extravagant claims about what they will do in office and the problems they will solve, and put forward solutions to problems which are completely unworkable in practice or which simplify complicated issues. But other people are taken in by it. So it is that people like Donald Trump, Boris Johnson, Jair Bolsonaro, and others acquire the role they crave.

At the same time, even when people in power have not deliberately manipulated others, and even if they were reluctant to take on the role, they often have unrealistic expectations projected onto them. People look for a COP meeting, or the G20, or the UN to save them. They expect their new president, prime minister, pastor or bishop to make everything right, and are disappointed.

5. Ideological filters

Karl Marx and others pointed out how those with power will deceive themselves and justify their position or their policies. It is not only those with power who suffer from self-deception, but theirs has the most obvious effect. Three examples will suffice.

Conservatives in Britain seem wedded to the idea that low taxation helps everyone because it releases money for investment and thus creates jobs and incomes, and that this is what people want. This is despite the fact that studies have shown that in the days of Reagan and Thatcher this 'trickle-down effect' did not work but simply increased the disparity between the very rich and the very poor, and that regular surveys show that people are happier in high-tax countries like Finland and Denmark than they are in low-tax countries like the UK and the US. Most people do not actually want more money in their bank accounts, they want public services that work.

Secondly, while in many ancient societies people valued things they did not actually need, this desire has been stimulated vastly since the Industrial Revolution, so that vast swathes of the world's economies are geared to producing things no one needs but can be persuaded to want. This process of production and consumption is so embedded in Western societies that it is not even noticed. It is just taken as the way things are. But consumerism is an ideology which is ecologically destructive and it will be defended vigorously by many industrialists and investors who benefit from the system, and who probably believe in it. Such self-deception has led many people to conclude that to seriously address the ecological crisis it is necessary to remove or radically change consumer capitalism.[3]

Thirdly, the history of the Soviet Union contains numerous examples of people being made destitute or dying as a result of agricultural and industrial policies introduced and enforced on the basis of Leninist ideology. Millions died because the new systems did not work, and scapegoats and critics were sent to the Gulag or executed.[4]

Western capitalists will be quick to point to the casualties of Stalin's collectivisation programme. But while the numbers of people who died in these disasters can be estimated, it is much harder to estimate how many have died in mines, factories, and desperate poverty to enable others to have cheap consumer goods. And it is impossible to estimate how many will die as a result of the ecological disaster to which consumerism is contributing.

All people have their frameworks within which they interpret what they see, hear or read. There is no neutral position from which to observe the ideologies of the world. Newspaper reporters select what they describe. Editors choose what to include and what significance to place on it. Historians choose what they tell, and how they tell it. Serious problems arise when people do not realise that they are interpreting the information according to their own values: if they are not aware that they hold a position, they consider their view to be absolute and see those who do not accept it as heretics, troublemakers, or enemies.

In the sixties and seventies one of the approaches taken by people working to liberate impoverished and oppressed people in South America was to practise 'conscientisation' through education. The aim was to help people see how the economic system worked against them, and how those with power were locked into it as well. It may be that the Green movement today has something to learn from this.[5]

6. Structures and systems

Reinhold Niebuhr also argued that those working for social justice were not just dealing with individuals but with corporations or organisations which had their own limited values. It was possible for someone in their family, neighbourhood or church to be seen as a 'good person' who at the same time supported injustice, discrimination, or violence through the organisation they worked for simply by going along with its aims or with the way it was structured.[6]

In the eighties, Walter Wink and others spoke about systems having a life of their own. Looked at this way, nations, banks, corporations, NGOs, etc. can be seen as much more than the individuals that comprise them. Using ancient mythological language, Wink called these things 'Powers'. The Powers, he said, can make a contribution to human flourishing but they also have a shadow side.

Wink also argued that domination systems, or Imperial Powers, reappear in different forms time and again, as if they reincarnate themselves. So it is that we can see many of the same dynamics within a modern multinational company as existed within the Roman Empire. The togas have been changed for grey suits, or jeans and tee shirts, but the lust for power and control remains the same.

Within such systems, or Powers, those who work for them might be oblivious to their downsides, or if they are aware of them, feel powerless to change them. And even those who appear to be in control have limited influence because of the dynamic of the system. So, when the leaders of nations gather in the UN, or the world's economic movers and shakers meet at Davos, they have less power than they would like others to believe, or possibly believe themselves. This means that people who look to them to save life on the planet by making radical decisions are often being unrealistic.[7]

7. Choices are seldom simple

Probably all of us at some time or other find ourselves in situations where we have to decide what to do but every option seems bad. There is no obvious right solution. There might not even be a best way, just a least bad.

It may be a small decision between whether to buy local food which is more expensive and have less money left for other essentials, *or* to buy something imported which has more food miles but enables the family to have more variety. Or it may be a big decision about whether to blow the whistle on an employer's malpractice and perhaps have difficulty finding further work, *or* to stay, have a decent income for the family and try to work within the organisation for change.

This tangled web of rights and wrongs is hard to navigate but that is how the world is much of the time. It calls for weighing up the pros and cons, making judgements, and accepting compromises. It is the situation that we as individuals in our employment and home life find ourselves in. It is also the situation of those who have the responsibility for making the big decisions concerning the future of their society, their country, or their corporation, and the future of life on the planet.

The people who make big decisions and policies are only people, whatever their pomp, style or wealth. Even if they are basically good people, they have their weaknesses, their shadows, their fears and memories, and their personal ambitions. Whatever they would like to see happen, they are pushed and pulled by various powerful interests. However much they might hear about what is happening in the world and what is at stake, their thinking is filtered by their own ideologies. And their power is not as great as others sometimes think because there are systems and structures beyond them. They are simply the visible parts of a complex invisible network of relationships.

Perhaps, in the light of all this, next time there is a climate conference or another major international convention, as well as lamenting what has not been achieved we might marvel if anything is achieved at all. And many things have actually improved for many people over recent decades. Some decisions have been made to tackle climate change, reduce pollution and plastic waste, to protect biodiversity and endangered species, and to support the world's poorest people. It is not as much as many of us would like, but it is not negligible.[8] There are also other aspects of being human which we do well to have in mind as we look for reasons to hope.

8. Emotion and compassion

In the nineties the subject of emotional intelligence came into management and educational discussions. This was a way of having in mind that people are not just thinking machines but that they have emotions and it is important for them and others to be aware of them. Without this awareness people can be easily manipulated or can act destructively.[9]

Politicians, advertisers, diplomats and campaigners have always been aware that often we base our decisions not on reason but on feelings. Work to produce peaceful settlements in situations of conflict has involved both 'hearts and minds'. Persuaders often appeal not to facts and reasons but to images and slogans which will make people feel a particular way. Sometimes the justification for a course of action may be put in terms of a logical argument but that is simply a justification of something that has actually been decided on the basis of what feels good, right or advantageous.

Recent psychological studies have identified a deep-seated emotional response which is sometimes called '*kama muta*'. This is a strong feeling of identification with another person or thing, and will surface as compassion or a sense of joyful oneness. This response has been found to be cross-cultural. It is not restricted to any gender or subculture, and is clearly a possible resource for creative action.[10]

9. Co-operation and altruism

Psychological research has also established that co-operation is a strong trait among humans. We are clearly not the only animals that co-operate but there is now strong evidence that it is not simply something that people do for their own individual advantage but is a deep-seated tendency. And it is easy to see why: a human being alone can do little so there is an obvious evolutionary advantage in people having a tendency to co-operate.

This runs counter to the prevailing idea of capitalism which is that basically people are individuals who are continually looking for their own advantage, or for the advantage of their immediate family or friends. This individualistic ideology is continually reinforced by practices within the capitalist culture but the evidence is that it is going against the grain.

More than that, there is widespread evidence of altruism. This ranges from people who give their time to help in food banks or charity shops, to people who are voluntary full-time carers, and to medics who give up lucrative professional practices to help others in war zones. Cynics will argue that these people get some return for what they do, mainly in a sense of feeling good, which is of course true, but that does not alter the fact that such activity takes place and is very widespread. Without it many of the people who are concerned only for themselves would not actually survive, or the society that benefits them would collapse.[11]

10. Cascades of change

The history of the last hundred years is a story of significant political, social and technological changes, many of which were not anticipated. For example, no one knows what will be invented. Vast resources are put into some fields of research and as a result sometimes great progress is made, but other significant discoveries have come by surprise: penicillin, stainless steel, and graphene, for example. No one anticipated the way that computers would develop, or genetic profiling, or mobile phones. Few people foresaw the collapse of South African apartheid or the Soviet Union, or the degeneration of American political debate and democracy.

In East Germany in the 1980s, prayer meetings began in several cities such as Erfurt and Leipzig. These meetings then grew to become major demonstrations against oppression by the Communist regime. Gradually the movement swelled until those in power realised they could not withstand the force of protest and agitation for change, and in 1989 there was a cascade of regime changes in a number of satellite states of the Soviet Union. As with any social change there were many causes, but some of these were small actions which galvanised other people to act.

The same can be seen in consumer society. The music industry, publishing and brewing are largely controlled by big corporations, but the work of small independent units has sometimes caused major changes to people's tastes and expectations. So it is that, working together, people produce changes and small changes can sometimes have big consequences.

The ecological crisis is complex. There are many competing interests and underlying issues, and there are no superheroes, only people. If we are to make constructive decisions and not be overwhelmed by the enormity of the challenges, we need to be able to find out and assess what is happening, and to do so in a time when misinformation is rife and the pressures to conform to the destructive norm are strong. To do that we need to have hope, even if we cannot be optimistic. And it is important to think about how we know what we know: how we make sense of the world we are part of.

Chapter 4

How we know:
Information, knowledge and wisdom

In a letter to Robert Hooke, Isaac Newton said, 'If I have seen further than others, it is by standing on the shoulders of giants.' Newton acknowledged his debt to the work of people who had gone before him and he corresponded with other scientists. He was a highly original thinker but recognised that he was part of a community. That is true to some extent of all of us, whether or not we are mathematical geniuses. We are part of communities but we also think for ourselves.

When we were born there was no one to tell us how to move our limbs, or what noises produced what result, or how the various shapes and colours we could see fitted together. If someone had tried to tell us we would not have understood. The sounds our ears received and transmitted to our brains made no sense to us until we made connections, and realised patterns. Slowly we learnt to see, to hear, to move, to speak and to understand. Adults played a part in this but initially, as young children, we worked most of it out for ourselves, because we had to.

We then developed as people by a mixture of innate ability, experimentation, and copying. How we move now is to some extent affected by what we saw other people doing when we were infants, and what they encouraged us to do. Similarly, we are born with the capacity for developing language but which languages we learn depend on what is spoken around us. Other people give us information, help us see connections, and enable us to develop skills. We acquire their values and ways of seeing things in a process of 'enculturation', becoming part of a culture, a society or a group with a shared language, values, and aspirations.

Other people influence us but they cannot do our thinking for us. As we watch television, listen to podcasts, read books and the Internet, see and hear new things, and as we have new sensual and emotional experiences, we put them with the mental patterns we already have and in so doing we change those patterns. We might sometimes have new ideas and we can 'change our minds', coming to see things differently.

The open mind

Some of the information we receive is unreliable. What people say to us or post on the Internet always has a particular slant and some of it is simply untrue. We have to find ways of checking the reliability of this information and we can do this in a number of ways: we can check out how it compares with what we have already decided is correct; see how it fits with what we already think; and we can check the sources of what we are reading or hearing. One reason books such as this have notes is so that readers can see that what they are reading is not just being dreamt up by the writer but has other sources which can be checked out.

As long as what we are told does not clash badly with what we already believe to be true we probably accept it. If it does clash, we might reject it as untrue, adjust or change what we already believe, or just hold on to it as a subject for further investigation.

Being able to think, rethink, and hold questions in our minds is a necessary part of growing as a person. Psychoanalyst Melanie Klein argued that very young children will see situations or people as either good or bad but, in time, will generally learn to see them as a mixture of both. This is a major mental and emotional development which helps them to live with the complexity of the world.

When adults are unable to accept such complexity, dangerous situations arise. They see other people as either for them or against them, and they may react violently to those who question their cast-iron certainties. But any manager, teacher or parent needs to be able to hold in mind that the people they are dealing with are neither perfect nor evil. They have their strengths, their weaknesses, their skills, their failings, their creativity, and their destructiveness. They are all complex and they can do both good and bad.

In trying to make sense of the world we need to be able to hold in our minds several possibilities as to what might be true, and a sense of the complexity of people. It is unhelpful to simply deny evidence or ideas which contradict or criticise our current understanding or practice. We sometimes have to keep an open mind until we are able to find out more, and then adjust our previous view or reject the new information as false.

Looking from different angles

Keeping an open mind is not the same thing as 'doublethink'. This phrase was coined by George Orwell in his novel *1984* to describe the deliberate corruption of language by an elite so that something could come to mean its opposite. War is peace. Slavery is freedom. Greed is good. All these are doublethink.

Doublethink is different from hypocrisy. Hypocrisy involves saying one thing while behaving in a way that contradicts it. Hypocrites sometimes deceive other people and also often deceive themselves. In moments of self-awareness most of us can probably recognise some hypocrisy in our own lives.

This is different again from 'cognitive dissonance': an uncomfortable condition which involves believing two contradictory things simultaneously, such as believing one's country is the epitome of democracy and yet also believing that the government is not what people have chosen; or knowing that people are being tortured and killed in war while also believing that there is a loving all-powerful god who could intervene if he chose to.

There are several ways of treating cognitive dissonance. One is to completely reject one idea as simply untrue. Another is to adjust or refine one or both ideas. A third is to reframe the disagreement to create a bigger, broader view of the situation which might involve seeing the two ideas as different angles on the same subject.

Looking at things from several angles is invaluable but not always easy. It features in physics, such as in quantum mechanics, and is very common in social sciences. For example, if a history exam question asks about the causes of the First World War any student who suggests that the war just had one cause would do badly. The question would need to be looked at in terms of politics, ideology, national identity, historical disagreements between France and Germany, attitudes such as national pride, and so on. Similarly, the different ways of understanding people which we considered in the last chapter can be treated as looking at the issue from different angles, rather than as necessarily competing explanations.

Checking out ideas

Scientists do not start from scratch but learn principles, skills and methods from other people, and inherit ideas and ways of seeing things. Any scientist needs to be able to live with the possibility of something contradicting their current thinking and not ignore evidence of it. Only then can they and others reach a better understanding, which may be a refinement of their idea, but may involve a completely new way of looking at things, bringing about a 'paradigm shift'.[1] Improved understanding can only come about if people are willing to countenance the possibility that they may be wrong. Or, at least, keep an open mind about things which do not fit their current way of making sense of the world.

Experiments and peer review are crucial to science. Experiments are carried out to gather more information, and are often designed to try to disprove an idea. Advances in science are generally made by someone coming up with a new or original way of interpreting a body of information and then testing it out. The aim is to test the theory to destruction and if it survives it is accepted.

Peer review works in a similar way. A scientist writes up their idea for other scientists to criticise, which they do by looking for logical inconsistencies, and by seeing how it fits with other ideas or insights which have already been robustly checked. In the ensuing debate the new theory might come to be accepted or be shown to be mistaken, or it may be adjusted to make it a better explanation. The twentieth-century scientist and philosopher Karl Popper argued that science works not by deduction from known facts but by someone having an idea which is then rigorously tested. And even if it fails, human knowledge is still advanced because this particular idea is now known not to be true.[2]

Scientific laws

Some scientific theories become so robust and reliable that they are deemed to be 'laws'. They are like landmarks from which a traveller with a map can work out the way to go. They are like the foundations of a building which we trust are sufficiently strong to hold up the whole structure.

Scientific laws do not, of course, *determine* what will happen but *describe* what will happen. The prediction is treated as a certainty. Scientific laws are reliable and applicable to different circumstances. They are fundamental to engineering and we rely on them continually in our use of technology. Whenever we cycle down a road we depend on the various scientific laws which have been used by cycle engineers, metallurgists and road designers, and which most of us cyclists know little about.

Scientific laws are treated as reliable but only in certain circumstances and within certain boundaries. For example, Newton's Laws of Motion were fundamental to the Industrial Revolution and the nineteenth-century development of technology and they are still fundamental to a lot of engineering work. However, at velocities approaching the speed of light or at the subatomic scale Newton's Laws of Motion are not accurate, and in those circumstances the insights of Einstein, Niels Bohr and others are employed.

Increasing complexity

Scientific laws are based on the principle that under identical conditions the same action will give the same results. However, real conditions are never absolutely identical and so, in engineering, for example, safety factors are built in to allow for anomalies and variations.

It all becomes more complicated when we are thinking about life. With living beings many other factors come into play, so there is more scope for random and chaotic behaviour. It is very hard, if not impossible, to predict exactly how a simple organism like a particular spirogyra, amoeba or fruit fly will behave in the next few seconds. With more complex plants or animals it is harder still.

Thinking about human behaviour becomes more complicated still. So many factors come into play that any simple solutions to human social problems are almost invariably wrong. Individual people do not always behave logically. Emotion, memory, deep-seated fears and desires, as well as interpersonal relationships, all come into play. Nevertheless historians, sociologists and psychologists look for patterns in human behaviour, such as those described in the last chapter, recognising that they cannot develop anything like the 'laws' that apply in physics.[3,4]

So it is that in thinking about human behaviour we can develop theories from the information available but we cannot conduct experiments of the rigour that is possible in physics or chemistry. We rely on making connections between what has happened in the past, and on the criticism and suggestions of others. Such 'peer reviews' are conducted in journals, in the columns of newspapers, in TV and radio discussions, and in conversations on social media or in pubs and cafés, and they are important. It is important to be open to the possibility that we may be wrong and to check out our ideas with others. We may have misinterpreted the data or there may be other relevant information we have not considered.[5]

Avoiding criticism

It is easy to develop wild and original ideas if we simply ignore information that does not fit the theory. This is one of the great sadnesses of much mental illness. Trying to help a paranoid person, for example, see that things are not as they seem is extremely difficult. Trying to tell them that they are mentally unwell is seen as another attempt to get at them.

Conspiracy theorists express their paranoia in public, sometimes using the megaphone of social media. Whether the theory is about paedophile rings in the circles of power, or 9-11 being instigated by the CIA, or Jewish plots to control the world, counter-argument is ignored or interpreted as support for 'the enemy'. In a period of social turmoil like the present time conspiracy theorists thrive. From all the available information, they choose what they need to convince themselves that there are simple solutions to complex problems and, often, someone to blame. They also do not check out possible misinformation, lies and fantasies.

Demagogues, dictators and bullies also avoid considering that they may be wrong. They gather around them people who will support their views and not question them. Sadly, some people are taken in by their bombast. In a time of anxiety people will clutch at straws, and grasp simplistic solutions if they are presented with confidence. So it is that wannabe dictators will sometimes fabricate or exaggerate problems, or even exacerbate or cause problems themselves, which they then blame on others while presenting themselves as the one to solve them.[6] This adds to the danger of our current situation; so the question of hope arises in thinking not only about the ecological disaster we face but also the social disruption that goes with it.

Knowledge and action

In ancient Greek there were several words which might be translated into English as 'knowledge'. One was *gnosis*, which was a secret knowledge: the kind of thing that only insiders know. Another was *poesis,* which was the knowledge that a skilled worker has which is learnt through the craft. There was *praxis,* which was an interaction of lived experience and reflection on it. And there was *theoria*, which was the activity of working to make sense of the world.[7]

We have been practising and thinking about *theoria* and we have not been doing so because it is the only kind of knowledge worth having but because our task demands it. We are trying to work out if there is a reasonable basis for hope in the face of the ecological crisis we are in. *Poesis*, whether it be in agriculture, art or technology is crucially important. As too is *praxis,* as social and political action needs to include reflection to be effective and creative. But once we stand back and ask what is going on in the world, and whether it is ultimately hopeless, we start to practise *theoria.*

However, for the Greeks, as for many other ancient peoples, such understanding was not sufficient for life. What was also needed was *sophia*, which is usually translated as 'wisdom'. The word 'wisdom' has not exactly dropped out of our language but it rarely features in our news websites, papers or social media posts. However, much of the pain of our present ecological crisis comes from its sheer foolishness, which is the opposite of wisdom. We are warming the planet. We know we are doing it. We know how we can change. But life and consumption goes on. It is utter foolishness to destroy the only place we have in which to live.

Philosophy

Philosophy means, literally, 'a love of wisdom'. For professional thinkers like Plato and Aristotle the way to wisdom was *theoria*. But in ancient societies there were people who were not among the social elite but who were also philosophers. Shepherds who wanted to know how best to look after their sheep, to understand the possible dangers of malnourishment or disease, how to anticipate changes in the weather, and deal well and fairly with their colleagues were, quite literally, philosophers. Parents who wanted to know how best to raise their children and get on well with their neighbours, including the cantankerous and the bitter ones, were philosophers. Carpenters who wanted to know how best to handle and use the various woods available to them, to train their apprentices in the craft, and to enable their businesses to thrive in difficult times, were philosophers.

Our lives may be very different from theirs but there are in many workplaces, families and communities, people who are informally recognised as ones who talk a lot of sense, whose opinion will be sought out, or whose decisions are trusted. Wisdom might come not only from *theoria* but also from *poesis* and *praxis*, from lived experience. So it might come to us from conversations and discussions in shops, offices, pubs, churches and cafés as well as in the work of poets, novelists, filmmakers, artists, dramatists, artisans, cartoonists, musicians, political activists, social workers, and scientists.

Wisdom is not about words but about life. It is an attempt to make sense of the whole of life, or of a small part of one's experience, to work out what one's attitude to the world and to other people should be, and how one should best act in particular situations. In the face of our society's current great foolishness we need to find and acquire wisdom. In the face of disaster we need hope. And in looking for wisdom and hope we would be foolish to ignore another aspect of human life, which is sometimes called 'religious experience'.

Chapter 5

A sense of something more:
The phenomenon of religious experience

No doubt people have always been intrigued or threatened by beliefs and practices different from their own. Some have wanted to understand them, some have wanted to learn from them, and others have wanted to destroy them. The systematic study of religions took off in the nineteenth century and from the beginning it has been controversial. For a start, there are people who do not like to see their particular practices and beliefs lumped together with those they consider mistaken or inferior.[1] The term 'religion' is also criticised as in its modern form it is a post-Enlightenment concept which is inappropriate in many situations.[2] Nevertheless, the academic discipline of 'Religious Studies' or 'Comparative Religion' continues and it is complicated.

It is simple enough to compare religious buildings, festivals, authority figures, scriptures, and so on, but that is of limited use. Not all Buddhists, for example, have the same attitude to temples, monastic orders, or prayer. Not all Jews have the same attitude to the Torah, Shabbat, or Israel. There are Christians whose attitude to the Bible is more like that of many Muslims to the Quran than it is to that of some of their fellow Christians. There are not only similarities and differences between religions but also significant differences within them. Many Muslims are desperately concerned because other people associate them with the actions of Hamas, the Taliban or the Iranian Revolutionary Guard when, in fact, they abhor them. And there are Christians who have to deal with colleagues who assume that they are anti-gay, when they are not, or believe that the world was made in six days, which they do not.[3]

The study of religious experience

One significant contribution to the study of religion was made by American philosopher and psychologist William James, who published a book called *The Varieties of Religious Experience* in 1902.[4] His aim was to describe, categorise and make sense of people's experiences which might be termed 'religious', by which he did not mean people's experiences of religion – exciting, boring, confusing, strange, or whatever – but their personal experiences that deeply affected them and were seemingly beyond the ordinary.

James's view was that these kinds of experience lay behind the development of religion, and there is surely some sense in that. Religion is not likely to have developed as a deliberate means of shaping people's view of the world, or as an exercise in answering big questions, or in order to create a system of rituals, rules and perhaps a professional workforce. All these things happened but the stimulus would have been the experiences of people.

There have been numerous individuals who have written about their mystical experiences, some of whom are perennially popular: Julian of Norwich, Teresa of Ávila, John of the Cross, and Hildegard of Bingen, for example. The Christian Churches alone have hundreds of such works, while many others will have disappeared without trace. Among Hindus, Buddhists, Sufis, and others there are many more. Later, in the twentieth century, German theologian Rudolph Otto published a seminal study of such experiences called *The Idea of the Holy.*[5]

However, important though such mystical experiences must have been, people's experiences of suffering, pleasure, birth, growth and death, plenty and famine, fear, hate and love, would also have played a significant part in the development of a society's beliefs and practices. New experiences and reflections would have contributed to and influenced the collective memories and narratives.

There is, of course, a relationship between a person's subjective experience and the religion they are already familiar with. As they try to understand and communicate their experience they will use familiar words and symbols. So while experiences generate and reshape religions, religions in turn influence how such experiences are understood and communicated.[6]

James based his work on other literature and his own work in psychology but he did not conduct what we would call 'fieldwork', although others have done so. In 1969 Alister Hardy set up a Religious Experience Research Centre at Oxford University. In 1982 the then director, David Hay, published the results of their work so far, in a book called *Exploring Inner Space*.[7] The conclusion was that profound experiences of an Other, the Sacred, or God, are widespread and are common among people who would not describe themselves as religious and who never or rarely attend a religious service.

Many of the people questioned in the research had never spoken about their experience with anyone else as they were afraid of being thought weird, so it was not that group pressure had somehow induced the experience. The people were of various ages and social backgrounds, and included men and women. Generally, their experiences gave people a sense of personal value and purpose. Instances of religious conversion were few and the experiences people described included not just what we might call 'mystical' but a sense of the presence of someone who had died, and premonitions.

Experiences of religion

In thinking about how widespread such experiences are we also need to include the sense of transcendence that someone might have while listening to music, be it in a cathedral, a concert hall or at an outdoor festival. The music might be classified as 'religious' but it might not. And we would also need to include a similar sense some people have while engaging with a piece of art, which again might be 'religious' art, but might not.

We would also need to include hauntings, and particularly the relief which might follow an exorcism. Also, speaking in tongues and the overwhelming sense that some Christians describe of being 'baptised in the Spirit', and of healings following prayer, the 'laying on of hands', or a visit to a shrine such as Knock or Lourdes. Also, the apparitions which people have experienced and which gave rise to the development of some of these shrines. It is, of course, the unusual or extraordinary nature of some of these experiences which leads to some people keeping quiet about them and to others declaring them as 'miraculous'.

It is also important to have in mind the far more common experiences of people within very ordinary religious situations. Within the Christian tradition these would include solidarity or fellowship with other believers, an occasional sense of another presence in prayer meetings or communion services, and of insight through the reading of scripture or other texts. There are places such as churches in which people sometimes experience a sense of peace, or depth. And there are what are sometimes called 'thin places' to which people sometimes feel drawn by something they cannot articulate: places such as Iona, Lindisfarne, Compostela, or Assisi. Such experiences are widespread across different cultures.

Everyday transcendence

In 1969 American sociologist Peter Berger published a short book called *A Rumour of Angels*.[8] His argument was that there are various aspects of human life which, while not 'religious' in the traditional sense, can still be seen as reflections of or pointers to something that transcends ordinary life: such things as play, hope, humour, and a conviction that there are some things which are absolutely wrong. His suggestion was that these things were 'signals of transcendence'.

We might want to add to this list the occasions when people discover within themselves resources they did not know they had, or a sense of a 'higher power' which they can draw on, such as in the 12-step process used by Alcoholics Anonymous and other addiction therapies. There is also the sense of wellbeing that some people acquire in nature, or in doing something good for others even at great cost to themselves; the sense someone might have that they are being drawn to doing something particular with their life; or a sense of gratitude for something good that has happened, even when there seems to be no one to thank.[9] Jewish philosopher Martin Buber, in his 1923 book *I and Thou*, wrote of deep relationships between people being fields in which the mundane is transcended.[10]

All these are aspects of human experience which it is hard to find a name for. They might be called 'religious', but that is problematic as much of this has little to do with organised religion. People often talk about being 'spiritual' without being religious, by which they probably mean they are aware of this aspect of life but do not engage in formal religious practices.[11] Whatever term we use, be it the Transcendent, the Other, the Holy, the Numinous, the Real, or the Spirit, it is surely not to be ignored when we are looking for reason to hope.

Fundamental questions

However, this raises a number of questions which we need to address, and we can do that by considering three common phrases.

'It's just imagination'?

Nothing is *just* anything. A tree not just a tree: it is a resting place for birds, host to thousands of insects, and a factor in the complex ecosystem of the soil, and it might be a break of deeper green in a garden, and a source of anticipation as it blossoms. Even a stone on the beach is not just a stone. It is a physical resistance to the weight of others around it; it is a remnant from a landslip along the coast, the product of millions of years of slow movement and compression, and of centuries rolling in the sea. In poetic mode someone could write twenty lines about a pebble on the beach. It is not just a stone. Everything is always many things, and imagination certainly is.[12]

Imagination is a source of great pleasure, a powerful tool in understanding the world, and a resource for reshaping it. Without imagination we would not have the Sistine Chapel, Mahler's 5th symphony, the Gaia Hypothesis, or the General Theory of Relativity. Albert Einstein famously began his exploration of relativity by trying to imagine what the world would look like if he was travelling at the speed of light.

Imagination enables people to think of things they have not seen or heard, and it is with imagination that people are able to conceive of other ways of organising their society, and to shape other futures for themselves. It is fundamental to social reforms and revolutions as it enables someone to say, 'It does not have to be like this.'

'It's all in the mind'?

The Sistine Chapel can be touched and measured but what impresses many people who visit it is not just the paint and plaster on the walls but something beyond the colours, shapes and patterns. There is something else about it, and that is what we have in mind when we think about experiences of transcendence. The question is: to what extent is that 'something else' in the viewer's mind and to what extent is it 'within' the picture.

If we play a piece of music through speakers the air in the room vibrates. These sound waves then cause vibrations in our ears which, if they are working well, translate them into electrical signals which our brains then interpret as sound. The music certainly has a physical aspect but what moves us about it is not just the sound, it is something else.

The effect of music on the human brain has been extensively studied.[13] The patterns of brain activity can be described, and certainly, they would be different for different people. For me, listening to Mahler's 5th is a pleasure, while for someone else it would be tedious, and no doubt those different emotions can also be detected as different brain activities. Our brains are turning the sounds into 'music', but they are not creating the music.

'There's nothing there, really'?

This is probably literally true. 'There' is a place, or a direction, and what we are talking about is probably beyond, or outside, direction. It transcends space and it is not a 'thing'. It is not a material object that could be measured, put in a container, or wrapped in paper. And this is a difficulty.

But the same applies to something like the Gaia Hypothesis. The plants, animals, air, clouds and solar radiation are all there and can be measured, and the connections between them can be watched, and analysed. But what about the hypothesis itself? That is a mental construct. It is an idea which rests in the minds of people. So to what extent is it real?

Similarly with Einstein's Theory of General Relativity. It was an idea in Einstein's mind as the result of numerous calculations, and he communicated it on paper and in lectures. Since he published it in 1916 numerous experiments have supported it. But the theory is not a tangible object. The theory itself cannot be measured, or moved, or touched, but does that mean it is not real?

Aspects of one reality

Materialism is the default setting in Western society. Not just materialism in the sense of wanting to acquire lots of stuff, but materialism in the sense of believing that matter is the fundamental characteristic of the universe: we are first and foremost bodies, the world is a ball of rock circling the sun, a tree is basically molecules formed into cells, a painting is fundamentally a mix of chemicals spread onto a woven fabric, and so on. The idea is that it is only matter that is real.

However, few people manage to live totally by the conviction that matter alone is real. We treat ideas and theories as real and talk about 'the Gaia Hypothesis' and 'the Theory of Relativity' as if they are objects in the same sense as the Sistine Chapel. Those of us who are principally concerned with matter, be it growing food, making furniture, or studying atomic particles, would still generally agree that it is things like friendship, love and beauty that make life worth living.[14]

There have been philosophical movements, often called forms of Idealism, which have reversed the emphasis, giving priority to what we might call the Transcendent. Plato and his followers believed that only ideas, in the sense of perfect forms, were the objects of knowledge and therefore only they could be said to truly exist. Through the European Middle Ages Neo-Platonism was very influential and the Church taught that what was most important was not the material world and the state of people's bodies but the state of their souls. In nineteenth-century Germany G.W.F. Hegel taught that everything was an emanation of a 'Universal Mind', while Platonism had a revival in England.[15]

But we could see the physical and the non-physical, or the material and the non-material as two aspects of a greater reality, like two sides of a coin.[16] As two aspects of one reality, they would affect each other. Or we could hold to a view that there are not just two but many aspects to reality, which are interrelated.[17]

This, surely, is how most people actually function, even if they do not formally subscribe to such a view. Idealists, however much they might prioritise ideas, thoughts or experiences of transcendence, are still influenced by their hormones and digestive systems. And dedicated Materialists still have musical preferences, appreciate good food, and fall in love. It might be argued that a fundamental characteristic of a good scientist is having a sense of awe at the world they are part of.[18] They certainly need to have endless curiosity and to want to see the world as it really is.

A need for caution

There is another concern that can emerge when we start taking the Transcendent seriously. The growth of materialism has had a liberating effect. As the scientific way of understanding of the world grew people became less fearful of demons, sprites, evil hexes and witchcraft. The stars and planets were no longer seen as strange and possibly malign forces that influenced human lives. Mechanisms replaced magic. If we start taking seriously the non-material aspect of reality will we not open the door to bugaboos and irrationality? This is a possibility.

However, we also need to have in mind that scientific materialism contributed to Auschwitz and Hiroshima, and is contributing to catastrophic climate change. The answer is surely not an outright materialism but taking seriously the material and the non-material aspects of reality. This is going to involve critique rather than gullibility, and, as far as possible, the use of a wide range of mental tools.

Recognising the reality and value of the non-material does not mean going back into a medieval or ancient world view but acknowledging that the material aspect is not the whole of reality. Acquiring wisdom from ancient writers will involve understanding their view and the context they wrote in and then interpreting their wisdom into our own time.

Chapter 6

Forms of ancient wisdom: Myths, poems, and parables

People have been engaging with and reflecting on the non-physical aspect of reality for millennia. Many ancient writers took it very seriously and in looking for wisdom and hope we will now turn to some of them. But, where do we start?

For anyone in Britain wanting to understand ecology the best place to start is probably not a forest in Borneo or the Appalachian Mountains but their own local park or garden, simply because it is nearest and they will already know it to some extent. On the same principle, when I decided during a dark period to investigate the question of hope, I reckoned that the best place for me to start was the place which was for me close to home: in the Hebrew and Christian scriptures. And that is where we will turn now.

This is not to suggest that there is not hopeful wisdom in other religious writings and practices such as the Tao-te-Ching, Zen meditation or Sufi stories, or in the holistic visions of First Nation Peoples of Australia or America, but we have to start somewhere. If the Hebrew and Christian scriptures provide something of what we are looking for we can then broaden our exploration. If they do not provide what we need we can look and maybe find it elsewhere.

But there is another reason for starting with these particular ancient writings, which is that they talk about hope. And while they were written in a very different culture from ours it may be that some of what they say, or claim, can be translated into our own culture and time. The writers, of course, did not have at their disposal the scientific and critical techniques that we can use, but they were not stupid. They survived, whereas we are not sure we will.

No one voice

There is an old Jewish joke that if you ask two rabbis for an opinion you will get three answers. The same could probably have been said of the Irish monks back in the days when Iona, Lindisfarne and Bangor were great centres of learning. And in the Hebrew and Christian scriptures there is difference of opinion, and a variety of views. This means that making sense of them is not a matter of trying to make a theoretical system out of everything they contain. Nor is it about joining together texts from different parts of the Bible. It is about listening into and perhaps mentally engaging in a dialogue.

Old Testament scholar Walter Brueggemann has used the model of a courtroom to interpret how the different voices in the Hebrew scriptures interact with each other. There is testimony but also dispute as other writers put forward alternative views. There is both argument and firm conviction.[1] New Testament scholar James Dunn, in the 1970s, highlighted how there is both considerable variety of opinion within the Christian scriptures, and common conviction.[2]

The origins of 'The Bible'

What Christians call 'The Bible', and which now usually comes in one cover, is two main collections of books. The largest by far is the Hebrew scriptures, or 'Books of the Old Testament', which consist of three smaller collections: the Torah, the Prophets and the Writings. The other is the Christian scriptures, which were written later.

The Hebrew scriptures were written over a period of more than eight hundred years, between about 1000 and 150 BCE. The Christian ones between about 45 and 110 CE. No one knows for sure. Neither is it known who wrote most of them and clearly many were the work of several authors, possibly over a long period of time. There were other books written in the same society and during that time, some of which are included in the Bible as used by the Roman Catholic Church but put in a separate collection called the Apocrypha by Protestants. Others were lost.

The writing probably began when twelve or so Hebrew tribes were united and established a political centre in Jerusalem around 1000 BCE. They called themselves 'Israel', built a temple, wrote songs and prayers, began to write laws and chronicles of events, and possibly began to write down the tales which had been told by their ancestors for centuries. They were never a significant player in the power politics of the Mediterranean and Middle East. They were on the route that campaigning armies took between Mesopotamia and Egypt and although for three generations they were a united kingdom they then divided and the northern part was wiped out by the Assyrians. The southern part, known as Judah and whose inhabitants became known as 'Jews', was taken over by Babylonians, Persians, Greeks and then Romans. For three generations, around 550 BCE, the Jewish elite were exiled in Babylon.

Despite, or perhaps because of, this they produced some remarkable literature. After these writings the Jews continued to collect and write commentaries, or *Talmud*, and sermons, or *Midrash*. The Christian offshoot from Judaism produced letters, gospels, and fantasy, some of which was eventually included in a definitive collection which they called the 'Books of the New Testament'.

What is in the collections

None of the writers of any of the books thought they were contributing to a big book called The Bible. They were writing for their own time, or perhaps the next generation. The idea that two thousand years later people would still be reading what they wrote would have blown their minds. And the way that some people now venerate their writings would have bothered them.

Despite there being a book called 'Numbers', in the Hebrew scriptures there is no mathematics. There is no science, in the sense of working by logic and experiment to understand how the world works. Neither is there any philosophy in the sense of arguing that if A is true, therefore so is B, and if that is true so is C. But there is plenty of philosophy in the sense of loving and looking for wisdom. A whole set of the books are often referred to as the 'wisdom writings'. 'Where is wisdom to be found?' asks Job. Another book is titled 'The proverbs of Solomon … for learning about wisdom'.[3]

There are letters, particularly in the Christian scriptures, and poetry, songs, proverbs, and stories. The stories range from tales which are completely made up to what may be fairly accurate reports of events. Many of them have in the past been called 'history' but that is not a simple term.

We assume that a book that purports to be history will contain factual information, although, even if it does, what is written has been selected from a mountain of material which could have been included. Authors have their own biases, honest interests and concerns. For an example of how history can be slanted try G.M. Trevelyan's *English Social History*,[4] which was published during the Second World War, and portrayed England as a jolly good place and suggested everything was slowly working together for the better. Or one of Arthur Mee's 'histories', which are still to be found in second-hand bookshops.

Such books as these can be described as giving a romantic view of the past. In England this is characterised by the idea of 'the good old days', as portrayed in *Downton Abbey* and a host of costume dramas. In Scotland it is characterised by Bonnie Prince Charlie, Rob Roy, and 'Flower of Scotland'. So we move from history to legend: legends being tales which probably have a historical core but have been so embellished by the teller's desire to entertain or influence that they become largely fiction, often with the core eventually being lost from sight and now impossible to substantiate.

The Armada happened, and historical research can reveal quite a lot about what actually took place, but it was not exactly as told in children's history books of fifty years ago. Sadly, Francis Drake, that paragon of English cool, was not playing bowls on Plymouth Hoe at the time. And Robin Hood, was he from Nottingham, or Barnsley, or even Whitby? However, he and his Merry Men are not only continually entertaining but provide a moral model or conundrum. Should one steal from the rich to support the poor, or simply introduce a tax on investment transactions?[5] And as for King Arthur, now allegedly sleeping until England needs him again, he has been the subject of many tales for centuries but is hardly a reliable ground for hope.

The power of myth

With such stories as Robin Hood and Arthur we move from history to 'myth', which is another word with various meanings. First, it is used for a story that is simply not true. 'Urban myths' are perhaps fun and possibly scary but they are supposed facts which are actually wrong. Secondly, the word is used to describe a story which shapes the attitudes and feelings of a group or society. As I write a million French people are taking to the streets to protest against proposed changes to their state pension scheme, and in their minds, perhaps operating unconsciously, is the story of the French Revolution. In the campaign to withdraw the UK from the European Union the so-called Brexiteers made references to Dunkirk, conjuring an image of plucky Britain once again not being cowed by bullying Europeans. The Revolution, Dunkirk, the Armada, Bannockburn all happened but they are more than simply historical facts.

The word 'myth' is also used for ancient stories which express a deep meaning. A mythopoeic society is one which explores the significance of things or the depth of life not with concepts and theories but with stories. As stories they are usually told as if they happened long ago but that is a literary device. For storytellers who believe the myth they are about the present time. The old Norse myths include gods like Odin, Freya and Thor, who are manipulative, argumentative and randy, and blunder around like the complex forces of wealth, sex, and muscle within a human society. The giant forces of rock and ice speak of an environment in which people struggle to survive with the help or hindrance of gods who have their own agendas. And the world tree, Yggdrasil, points to the interconnection of all life. Ancient Greek myths have provided later Western psychologists with concepts or models to understand the human mind and emotions, but they were about more than the human mind. Even when some philosophers were questioning their existence, many people saw Eros giving a creative or disruptive charge to community life, Nemesis waiting to cut down those who overstepped their limitations, and furious Ares wreaking havoc and destruction in the frequent wars between states.[6]

Modern literary genres which sometimes operate in a similar way to myth are science fiction and fantasy. Some science fiction and fantasy writings and films are simply intended to entertain and sell, but not all. Writers such as Ursula Le Guin and Isaac Asimov were deliberately using their fantasies to explore issues and raise questions and awareness. J.R.R.Tolkien was a philologist and scholar of medieval literature who drew on the imagery within it to develop his Middle Earth fantasies, aware that he was doing more than telling entertaining tales. Many people find Terry Pratchett's Discworld novels hugely entertaining, and he wrote them for fun, but within them he also explored some significant social issues.[7]

A wealth of metaphors

In a bookshop or library, books will be classified and sometimes it is easy to decide which section a book belongs in. But classification is not always clear. Does Terry Pratchett's *Thief of Time* belong in fantasy, humour, philosophy, or social criticism? Usually 'fantasy', but it contains them all. Does Ursula Le Guin's *Wizard of Earthsea* belong in fantasy or psychology? It will normally be put with 'young adult fiction' although in a story set in an imaginary world it explores theological, ecological, and psychological themes.

In ancient literature the categories are often far from clear. It was not an issue to the writers, and rarely to the editors and compilers. So, even more than in many modern writings, one book may contain many genres of literature, shaken, stirred and mixed. One such significant genre is poetry with its creative use of similes and metaphors.

Similes are simple. *This* is like *that*. 'Like a bridge over troubled water …' (Paul Simon, 1970) or 'Like a rolling stone …' (Bob Dylan, 1965). But metaphors are more subtle and often more powerful. In a metaphor one thing is used to refer to something else that is like it in some respects, although perhaps not in an obvious way. 'The answer is blowin' in the wind' (Bob Dylan, 1963). 'I am a rock, I am an island …' (Paul Simon, 1965).

A good poet will conjure up new metaphors or use old ones in imaginative ways, and when reading old poetry we can still be excited or enlightened by metaphors even when they are familiar. But sometimes metaphors die. This is not always a problem. In fact, it can be quite useful in ordinary speech. We talk about the *leg* of the table, the *chair* of a council, or a *board* meeting, without realising they are all metaphors. In science we talk about an electric *current*, a magnetic *field*, and the *charm* and *spin* of subatomic particles. Metaphors are useful, and particularly so when we are trying to describe something that is not material.

Out for a meal recently at a local pub I read what the menu said about a particular Spanish wine: 'Elegant, very rich palate, fleshy and well structured. Fresh and acidic mid-palate highlights subtle varietal character, enhanced by some fruity notes. Fresh and intense finish.'[8] Where would wine aficionados be without metaphors? Or theologians, who try to think and talk about subjects even more subtle than the taste of a wine?

The Hebrew and Christian scriptures are rich in metaphor. Some of it is prosaic, but much is vivid. And some of it dies but still remains very useful as a way of speaking about the transcendent, mysterious Other with which or with whom the writer was ultimately concerned.

Verbal art

There are also parables in the Hebrew and Christian scriptures. Jesus was, of course, one of the most famous tellers of parables but they feature in many other cultures. Parables are usually short, but not necessarily so, and are fundamentally a way of talking obliquely about something. They enable a teller to make a point without spelling it out and in so doing they make the hearer think and remember. A parable is not a bald statement, it is a small piece of art which can be thought about and reflected on in different ways. It is not an allegory in which one thing always means another in such a way that the story can be deciphered. Parables work away in the mind like a picture, a joke, or a good song.

A parable might have one basic point, but not always.[9] Some of

Jesus' parables, such as the Mustard Seed, or the Lost Coin, might, but parables such as the Prodigal Son or the Sower can be heard in many ways.[10] This is true in the Hebrew scriptures too. The prophet Nathan told a very sharp story to King David which made David condemn his own actions and enabled Nathan to criticise the king and survive. But the story of Jonah, which is also a parable, has many themes.[11]

Someone telling a story is rarely dressing up an idea or a point in a piece of entertainment but creating a work of verbal art to be heard, reflected on, remembered, and often acted upon. What this means for scriptures as a whole is that in reading them we are often not dealing with bald statements of purported fact but with rich and subtle stories, with powerful poetry, with proverbs, songs, and visions. We are often not dealing with propositions but with art.

Part 3

ANCIENT WISDOM

Chapter 7

Creation:
Genesis, Psalms, Isaiah

In the dark an elderly priest is sitting on the bank of a great river. A mist hangs over the water so he can see nothing except the swirl and wash at the river's edge. He has been weeping but is past tears now. For the last few days he has been hearing the laments of the people.

'How lonely the city sits that once was full of people'[1]

'How can we sing the Lord's song in a foreign land?'[2]

By the waters of Babylon the people lay down and wept when they remembered Zion. Jerusalem was now destroyed. The great temple in which the priest had worked was now rubble, with the place of God, the Holy of Holies, trampled by unbelieving soldiers. The people's inheritance has been turned over to strangers and the people now are like orphans.[3]

As he half-watches the water he becomes aware that he can now see something more. There is light, and slowly he can distinguish the land from the water and see the reeds and willows on the banks. A dawn wind moves the mist and above him he can see a dome of stars which slowly fades as the east grows bright and then the sun rises above the horizon. Birds take to the air from their roosts. Dragonflies hover over the shallows, and there are more sounds. Cattle are being taken to drink. Herdsmen are talking. And he has an idea.

The priest now has a poem. A story. A message.

'In the beginning God created the heavens and the earth', it begins. 'The earth was a formless void and darkness covered the face of the deep, while a wind from God swept over the face of the waters. Then God said, "Let there be light", and there was light.'[4]

And in the poem God calls the world into being: land, plants, sun, moon and stars, birds, insects, fish, and finally animals and humans.

Creation story

I do not know if that is how the poetic story that begins the book of Genesis actually came to be written. Probably not. I wrote that, adapting a story I heard years ago and which I have told and altered many times. That is what happens with stories.[5]

No one knows who wrote Genesis 1, but someone wrote it, and perhaps they were inspired by the dawn. It is the first book in the Bible but it was not the first thing in the Bible to be written, by any means. It was put at the beginning because it sets the scene for what follows.

It seems that it was written during the Jews' Exile in Babylon, and also that it was written by a priest, or someone with an interest in and sympathy with the things that priests did. Over a century ago scholars looked at the first five books of the Bible, the *Torah* as Jews call them, or the *Pentateuch*, as Christian scholars call it, and realised that they were made of many strands woven together. The different strands came from groups or individuals which had different views, interests, styles and outlooks. One strand was the priestly strand, and the opening section of Genesis is in that style.

Another strand spoke a lot about *Yahweh*, the god of Israel, who liberated the people from slavery, made a covenant with them, and led them into a land of their own: a land from which, by the time the opening story was written, their leaders, priests and intellectuals had been removed.

Another strand talks more about 'God': *El* or *Elohim*. 'Elohim' is a strange word. It is definitely singular, but has a plural form. The Arabic word *Allah* is related to the Hebrew *El*, in the way that the English word 'God' is related to the German '*Gott*'.

In some of the older poems and stories of the Bible it seems as if Yahweh is thought of as simply one among several gods, albeit the one who has chosen Israel as his people. But over time there grew a sense that Yahweh was El. In the Exile it grew even stronger: that Yahweh was the only God. There was One God, who was Yahweh, Elohim, and all others were false gods: non-gods. And the One God called everything into existence.

The author of Genesis 1 was not the only biblical author who spoke of God creating the world. The night sky, so clear in the dry Middle Eastern air, was a cause of wonder, and according to Psalm 19 it was 'God's handiwork', and Psalm 8, 'the work of God's fingers'. In the book of Job, after much discussion and debate, Job is silenced by God commanding him to consider the world around him, all of which God has created. Isaiah 40, also written during the Exile, says, 'The Lord is the everlasting God, the Creator of the ends of the earth.'[6]

Crucial question

Monotheism was not new. In Egypt there had been an attempt by Akhenaten to establish monotheism. Some Indian scriptures suggested that there was a God beyond the many gods. The idea of a distant, supreme God was widespread, but the God was usually thought to be uninterested in the affairs of mere humans. However, in Hebrew thinking during the Exile, the Creator was also the One who had rescued the Israelites from slavery and made a covenant with them, and whom they had, with varying degrees of devotion, worshipped since then.

For people who believe that there are gods it is important to know what a particular god is concerned about and how it operates. Then you can know how best to behave in their area of influence, and what they want in order to work for your good. This applies whether it is Freya, Aphrodite, or Sex; Thunor, Demeter, or the Economy; whoever or whatever.[7]

If someone believes that there is just One God, the crucial question is what this God is like: what matters to the God, how the God relates to the world, and how people should behave in the light of this. There could be two neighbouring tribes who both believe there is One God, but if one tribe believes God is concerned about position, power, and destroying the opposition, while the other believes God is concerned about each individual and wants them to live and work harmoniously, the members of these tribes will see the world differently and act in different ways. The Hebrews identified God as the One whose concerns were made known in the Torah, the words of the prophets, and the wisdom writings of Israel.

Myth and science

Alhough it is not the only passage in the Hebrew scriptures which speaks of God 'creating' the world, Genesis 1 is probably the most well known, and as a piece of mythological poetry, it is very powerful.[8] It is myth in the sense that it has shaped people's view of world. Also, though it tells a tale as something that happened, it is about now. It is not about history but about the present. It is not about how things were but about how things are. It is not science or history but poetry.

It was a tragedy that when the scientific method was developed and refined there were not enough influential Christians who had the literary sense to realise that a scientific paper and the opening of Genesis were two completely different genres. This failure has meant that for a century or more many Christians have ignored the opening of Genesis because they find it embarrassing or they did not want to have an argument with the literalists, and its relevance for human life is therefore ignored. There are still millions of Christians who cannot let go of the thought that what is told in Genesis is history.[9]

Full of wonder

Clearly, in the poem the world is structured in the way the writers believed it to be. They could not have done otherwise. Later we will address the issues that might arise for us of having a very different view of the structure and dynamics of the universe, but for now we will note some of what the poem says.

Time and again the poem says, 'God saw that it was good.' Fundamentally, it is saying, the world is 'good'. It is not saying that it is free of pain and death, always pleasant, or always bright and beautiful, but that it is not fundamentally a threat, or evil. This was a significant assertion to make in a society where farming was a laborious struggle with pests and weeds, surgery was rudimentary, there were no antibiotics and very few painkillers.

Also, the world is a creation. It is like a great sculpture, a piece of music, a magnificent building, or a dance. It is full of wonder and beauty. And though the Hebrew writers do not wax prolific about the beauty of the world in the way that European Romantics or some ancient Celts might have done, they appreciated it: the trees, birds, mountains, rocks, flocks of sheep and fields of corn.[10]

What is not there

It is worth noticing what is not there in Genesis 1 or in the other references to creation in the Hebrew and Christian scriptures. There are none of the angels, archangels or demons beloved of medieval artists and the likes of John Milton. Neither are there any other gods, nor angels. It seems that angels came into Jewish thinking after the Exile when Persian power and culture were very influential, appearing in the final edits of the Hebrew scriptures and enabling people to talk about God interacting with people without actually saying or thinking that it was God directly. 'Angel' is a Greek word which means simply a messenger.

God creates 'the heavens and the earth'. That is everything. God is One. God creates everything. It is unclear whether the writer intended to convey, or even thought, that 'before' the Creation there was nothing. Christian theologians have generally held that the Creation is indeed *ex nihilo*, as they say, but whether that was in the writer's mind is not clear. Perhaps it was inconceivable to them. But even so, what the writer did describe as being at the beginning was empty, formless and dark. There was nothing to grab hold of. Nothing to touch, or see, or feel. There was no thing. Effectively nothing.

The spirit of God

Across this ocean of chaos moves 'the spirit of God'. Or 'a wind from God'. Or even 'a great wind'. Spirit, breath and wind are all the same word in Hebrew, as they are in Greek. The breath of a person is essential to their life. When they die they stop breathing: their breath, or spirit, leaves them. Here in Genesis the spirit or breath of God moves over the chaos before God calls light into being.[11]

Which word is best to use in translating or retelling this story depends on how people will hear or read it. In older Hebrew poetry there was talk of the hand of God, God's strong arm, God's feet, God's heart, and so on. This came from the Hebrew way of thinking and talking about a person as a whole, with particular aspects of a person being identified with parts of the body.[12]

In time, while Jews would have been reluctant to talk about God in that way because it sounded as if they thought God had a body, which God clearly did not, the term 'breath' or 'spirit' remained. Spirit remained as a very rich and useful metaphor. The image in Genesis 1 is of a great wind moving over a rough sea: the life of God hovering over chaos.

Although it may have become a dead metaphor, the word 'spirit' is valuable and crops up elsewhere in the Hebrew scriptures. In Psalm 104 the writer describes the world and its wonders including the wild animals, great trees, nesting birds, and people. But, says the writer to God, 'When you hide your face they are dismayed; when you take away their breath they die. When you send forth your spirit (or breath) they are created, and you renew the face of the ground' (Psalm 104.29–30).

While God is beyond the world and calls it into being, God's spirit or life is also among the creatures. The spirit of God is the source of their own life, and the source of new life. It is an image used very powerfully by the prophet Ezekiel in a famous story of a valley of dry bones which come together into bodies at the prophet's command, but only come to life when the wind or spirit enters them.[13] Isaiah speaks of how the spirit of God is upon him and has anointed him to bring good news to the poor.[14]

Time and again in the Hebrew scriptures God 'speaks'. God expresses Godself,[15] usually through prophets. In the early days there were clearly charismatic prophets who wandered in bands and sometimes spoke from a trance-like state, but the writings of later prophets were forthright, clear statements, often expressed in well-crafted poems,[16] or in powerful and imaginative stories[17] with a rich association of words and ideas,[18] or in dreamlike visions.[19] One way or another God expresses Godself. And according to Genesis 1, God does that in the very act of creation. God says, 'Let there be light …'

The One

Put all this together, and we have a concept of One who is beyond everything but also within the Creation, and who expresses Godself in many different ways. This gives a picture of the world, God's creation, as being within God. Or of God permeating and transcending the cosmos, while actively engaging with it.

This idea about the world gives rise to at least two kinds of issue for us with our understanding of our small place in a vast expanding universe, and in the face of a human-induced ecological disaster. There are what we might call cosmological problems, such as how we think about the world, and how we might think about it in relation to a Creator God. There are also what we might call ethical issues, such as how, if the cosmos is created by God, there can be such suffering and such a threat to life. We will return to those issues as they are both very relevant to thinking about the crisis we face and what hope there might be. But first we need to look at what else these scriptures say about God and humanity.

Chapter 8

God and humanity:
Genesis, Psalms, Amos, Micah

Perhaps Bible scholars would be helped by telling more stories. In the story of the battle of Jericho why do the Israelites march round the city blowing their horns for six days? Tell it to a class of primary school-children and you find out. The mounting tension is palpable. Then there is Gideon laying his fleece, or Moses trying to get out of the job God wants him to do. They are all good drama.[1]

The same goes for Genesis chapter 1. After making a world full of living creatures God pauses and mulls over what to do next. Then God says, 'Let us make humankind in our own image' (Genesis 1.26). It is the climax of the story and the timing is excellent. Perhaps if a dolphin or an octopus was telling the story they would put their species last. In the story we have, the human story, it is humans who are last. It is great storytelling but it has had the unfortunate consequence of Bible-reading humans thinking of themselves as the pinnacle of creation.

Humanity

'Let us …', says God. Perhaps it is bad editing of an earlier story in which several gods made humanity. Perhaps it is just that the strange plural singular word 'Elohim', God, requires a plural verb. But possibly it is just what people do when they talk to themselves. 'Let's have a beer!'

Whatever the reason, humanity is called into existence. Male and female together. No priorities. No hierarchy. Kings are not made first and then minions to serve them. Humanity as a whole: male and female, to be the 'image of God'. Made 'in God's likeness'.

This phrase has caused untold damage, although we probably should not blame the writer. The problem has partly been that people have read into this phrase what they wanted to see. Machos have seen it as meaning that as God is strong, they in their toughness are godlike. Creatives have emphasised God's creativity, while the intelligentsia, knowing God to be brighter than everything else, have seen themselves as closest to godness.

The word translated 'image' means, literally, a picture or statue. A representation. But we are dealing here with metaphor. It is poetic myth so is not to be taken literally, but it is suggesting some sort of likeness between humanity and God. Humanity is, or is to be, in some sense like God.

Whatever that likeness is it would mean that God would have a creature like Godself with whom God could have a relationship which is more than that of creator and product. It would also mean there was something to show the rest of creation what God is like. As 'an image of God', humanity was to be both a correlative to God and a representation of God.

Dominion

The difficulty of interpreting the phrase 'image of God' has not been helped by being linked with the word 'dominion'. God said, 'Let us make humankind in our image, according to our likeness; and let them have dominion over the fish of the sea, and over the birds of the air, and over the cattle, and over all the wild animals of the earth, and over every creeping thing that creeps upon the earth' (Genesis 1.26–27).

The concept of 'dominion' is not unique to this passage in Genesis. In Psalm 8 the writer marvels at the night sky, ponders humanity's place in the cosmos, and asks, 'What are human beings that you are mindful of them, mortals that you care for them? Yet you have made them a little lower than God, … crowned them with glory and honour … and given them dominion over the works of your hands' (Psalm 8.5–9).

The writer was marvelling at humanity's power in the world and saw that as a God-given fact. For them it was not an aberration that people were able to sleep without continual fear of predators, to look after sheep, goats, chickens and cattle and not have to continually search and hunt for food. That was how things were and it was good. It was a blessing, so God was to be praised for it.

However, two problems arose within the Judaeo-Christian culture for whom these writings became holy scripture. One was that technology improved beyond the potter's wheel and the iron-edged plough to steam power, the internal combustion engine, electricity, atomic power, and on to space exploration, genetic modification, and artificial intelligence. The other was that people forgot that with power goes responsibility. They were to be the image of God but, according to the Hebrew scriptures, being like God is not about having unbridled power, or being hyperintelligent, or supercreative.

Time and again prophets tried to tell or remind people what God was like, or, more to the point, what mattered to God. Elijah stood up against King Ahab's abuse of his power in taking a vineyard from one of his subjects.[2] Amos declared that God despised the music and worship of the Israelites because what he principally wanted was justice. 'Let justice roll down like the waters, and righteousness like an everflowing stream' (Amos 5.24). Micah said to people, 'What does the Lord require of you but to do justice, and to love kindness, and to walk humbly with your God?' (Micah 6.8).

Although they come later in the Bible these prophets predate the writing of Genesis 1 and would probably have been known to the writer. They describe what being the image of God and having power means. And this is what humanity has not done, and the consequences are now disastrous.

What humanity has also failed to do is to recognise the world, the earth, the cosmos, as a creation. While people are shocked and horrified when a protestor throws paint on a Van Gogh, or disrupts a concert, they think little of God's creation being trashed. The earth is not seen as a wonder to be marvelled at, as the writers of Genesis and Psalm 8 and many other ancient peoples saw it, but as a resource to be exploited.

Independence

There is something else in this poem of Creation which is significant but is easy to miss, perhaps because it is familiar or it is too obvious. God calls the world into being. The world is not an emanation of God and neither is God spinning a body for Godself. The world is seen as having an independence of God. And humans, 'the image of God', are to have a relationship with God and to show God to the world. They are not puppets. They are not controlled.

It is like starting a painting or drawing from imagination. You do not know when you start how it will end up. A novelist invents a character but the character begins to take on a life of their own. Writing a poem often begins with simply the first phrase and then it develops, possibly going into a theme that the poet did not anticipate, and images emerge as the writing goes on. A composer starts with a theme and develops it.

Even with a simple song the writer will almost be feeling their way forward to find the right word or chord. Yet it is not 'right', in an exact sense. There are different words or chords that could be used, and they would take the song in a different direction and give it a different feel, although there are many that simply would not work at all. So too with a story. There are many possibilities but there also needs to be continuity and consistency for it to be coherent and credible. Even a fantasy story needs inner consistency for the reader to be able to suspend disbelief and enter imaginatively into that fantasy world. Many things are possible, but not any thing.

Down the centuries philosophers and theologians have struggled with questions of freedom and determinism. The Hebrews were not much given to that kind of abstract philosophising: they talked about God speaking and acting, not about who or what God was in Godself. Here in Genesis 1 the writer addresses the matter of freedom, dependence and determinism not with abstractions but in a poetic story, in which the world and all that is in it is God's creation.

Other stories

This opening creation story is followed in Genesis by a sequence of much older stories. They are mythological but strung together to make a chain of prehistory for the later stories of the Hebrew patriarchs. Some are long, others very short, and some give tantalising glimpses of other stories now lost.[3] There are also purported genealogies which are rather like those of ancient kings in other myths who saw themselves as descended from gods, except that in Genesis humanity is not descended from a god but created by God.

Humanity is made from clay, dust, or soil in Genesis 2. It is an old image which occurs in other mythologies. In many cultures when a person dies they are put back into the ground and become earth again. In this Genesis story God shapes a man out of clay and breathes into him, and, it says, he becomes a 'living being'.[4] He is not a body with a soul but a living entity: a whole. There is no soul- or mind-body dualism, but the Hebrew concept of life was holistic, and life came from the breath, spirit, or wind of God.

The story plays with the Hebrew words for ground, *adamah*, and man, *Adam*. It then goes on with another play on words and God making woman from man. It was a patriarchal society so, not surprisingly, the man comes first, but the man describes the woman as 'flesh of my flesh and bone of my bone' (Genesis 2.23). Perhaps this is an attempt at balance, especially as everyone knows that a man is born of a woman. There is no suggested inferiority or subjugation built into the Creation. The story also has echoes of human attraction and sexual unity.

Then within the narrative are four big stories: the Garden, the Two Brothers, the Flood, and the Tower. These are mythical explorations of how things are in human life. They are not allegories, and they are certainly not history, but behind them is human experience.

The man and woman are put in a garden, and it is like an ideal childhood.[5] Everything is provided. There are no worries. There is an instruction with no explanation, but with a threat. They can go where they like and eat what they wish but if they even touch one particular tree they will die. A crafty snake comes along and tells the woman that if she ate the fruit she would not die but would have divine knowledge of good and evil. That is, she would know what is good or harmful to humanity. And knowing, to Hebrew thinking, was not just a matter of having a correct idea but was also a matter of experience.[6]

What happens is well known. The woman eats some fruit and gives some to the man. The snake is right. They do not die. But they see things differently. They feel shame and become self-conscious in each other's presence, and in God's. They are banned from the garden to an adult world of hard labour and painful childbirth, and there is no going back. We sometimes wish we could go back to a time when we were looked after, where everything we needed was provided, where there was no stress, no worries, and we were always safe. Or we might feel that there was once a time in our past when everything was good but we, by our actions, spoilt it. However, in this story, God is not harsh and makes clothes for the man and woman to protect them in the harder world in which they would now live and die.

How life is

The Two Brothers[7] is a story about sibling rivalry and also reflects the age-old struggles between nomadic herders and settled farmers. In jealousy, the settled farmer Cain kills his brother Abel, but God knows and condemns Cain to a life of wandering. God does not condemn Cain to death and even gives Cain a mark so that people will see he is still protected by God.

However, human society becomes violent and in exasperation God decides to do away with them all, except for one good man Noah and his family.[8] So there is the famous and terrible story of a flood over the whole earth and Noah cooped up in a box with two of all the animals of earth. An ark is a box, not the pretty little boat of children's pictures. But finally the flood subsides, the family leave the ark, and they repopulate the earth.

Finally, before the stage clears and the narrative focusses on nomadic Abraham and his descendants, there is the Tower.[9] A new technology has been developed and, with clay bricks and bitumen adhesive, the people of Babel build a tower with the aim of reaching heaven and thereby acquiring godlike status. So it goes on today, not only with unnecessary towers from Canary Wharf to Kuala Lumpur but with space ventures, cruise ships, gene editing, and AI. 'We can do it so we will.' In Genesis, hubris is another human trait. The tower of Babel is destroyed, the people are scattered across the earth, and their language is confused.

These are wonderful, rich stories about how life is. They are myths.

Treating them as history, as has often been done, and as some people still do, fails to recognise the kind of literature that they so clearly are, and often misses the depth, or even the point. Treating them as history also bristles with problems. Snakes do not talk, and it was a snake in the story, not a demonic being called Satan. And where did these other people come from who were going to be a threat to Cain? Or his wife? Were there supposed to be two of each animal or seven that went into the ark?[10] How did they all fit in? Where did all the water come from? And where did it go? And so on. Sadly, while children know a good story when they hear one, some adults set off to look for remains of Noah's Ark on Mount Ararat.

Sin and Fall

One reason some Christians are determined that these stories must be history is because they are wedded to the idea of a Fall. That is, man and woman were immortal until they sinned by eating the fruit in the garden and their sinfulness is now passed on down the generations. This leads to all the evil we see in the world, which was perfect before the Fall, and means that every human stands under the condemnation of God.

This idea of a Fall appeared in Jewish writings shortly before the time of Jesus, in the second book of Esdras, which is not included in the Hebrew or Christian scriptures. In the gospels Jesus talks about people being wicked, or evil, but this is Jewish hyperbole. Jesus' sayings and parables are full of such overstatements and stark contrasts. Paul picked up the idea of a Fall in his letters when he spoke about 'sin' as if it was a power that had hold of people. But it moved centre stage in Western Christian theology in the writings of Augustine of Hippo.

What developed was a whole theory of inherited sinfulness, passed on by sex. We were saved by Jesus dying on the cross to pay for our sins and his spirit could help us overcome our innate sinfulness. There were various ways of helping that to happen, and one was avoiding sex, hence an emphasis on celibacy among priests, monks and nuns. This schema is a long way from the attitude of the Hebrew scriptures. It is heavily influenced by a Greek dualism of body versus soul, and by Manichaean beliefs about the world being evil. The idea of a payment is enhanced by northern European pagan ideas about honour and wergild.

Augustine's views were criticised at the time and subsequently. It has been pointed out that it is unjust to condemn someone for what they have inherited. It is also unreasonable to tell someone to do something that they are constitutionally unable to do: that is a form of bullying. And also, believing that we are inherently weak and sinful can be an excuse for not trying, like an alcoholic continuing to drink because they do not believe they have the power to stop. Or, people not doing anything about their carbon footprint because they think they cannot manage without their large car and their cruises.[11] However, Augustine also had a point.

As we noted in chapter 3, we do not have absolute freedom about what we can do. We are very constrained by our physical nature, our background, our expectations, our mindset, our emotional baggage, and the systems in which we operate. And much of this is inherited.

Grace

There is a fear in some Christian circles that if they deny that there was a historical Fall the whole edifice of Christian doctrine will collapse. Far from it. To say that there was no historical Fall, and that 'original sin', as some theologies call it, is not passed on like a biological characteristic, is not to ignore the fact that we are restricted, damaged, and have ways of behaving which are destructive to ourselves, other people and the world. We will return to this issue but let us note for now that running through these ancient stories is a sense of what Christians call God's 'grace'.

The theme of God caring about humanity, even when they have done great wrong, runs like a thread through the Hebrew myths and legends. The characters in the scriptures are not perfect, and even some heroes behave appallingly. Noah gets drunk and shames his family. Abraham tells the Egyptian Pharoah that his wife is actually his sister and lets Pharoah add her to his harem for a while. King David seduces or rapes another man's wife and then has the man killed. Solomon becomes a tyrant. Elijah wants to give up on life. Elisha is a grumpy old man and curses some mocking children.[12] These are just some of the bits which are left out when Bible stories are told to children. But in these stories, despite their behaviour, God still cares about the people.

Grace is unearned goodwill and it is very common. It is what we expect parents to have for children, who should not have to earn their meals or do something special to have a hug. Good neighbours do things not expecting a favour in return. When someone provides hospitality to someone in need, when a country provides food and shelter for a wave of refugees, or a medic gives their services for a low wage in a war zone to help people they do not know, that is grace. It is the attitude and action that we see in God time and again in these scriptures.

It is here in the clothes God makes for the man and woman, the protective mark on Cain, the Ark, the ongoing life of humanity despite its violence and hubris. And there in that first story-poem of the creation of all things: the whole, mysterious, interconnected, living world called into being by God is a result of grace. As the narrative continues, God's grace becomes even more clear.

Chapter 9

God's freedom:
Exodus, Proverbs, Amos, Micah

The story goes that Moses was looking after his father-in-law's sheep when God spoke to him. The background was that the Israelites, or Hebrews, the descendants of Abraham, Isaac and Jacob, who was also called Israel, were now enslaved in Egypt.[1] Moses was an Israelite who had grown up in the royal court, had killed an Egyptian slavemaster, and had then run away to the wild lands of Sinai hoping for a quiet life. That worked out until one day he was fascinated by a burning bush, and as he approached the bush God spoke to him.[2]

God told Moses that he was on holy ground and should take off his shoes, which Muslims now do when they enter a mosque. But the shoes were not the big issue. What God then said was that he had heard the cries of the Hebrew slaves and had come down to rescue them from their slavery. And he, Moses, was to lead them.

This story, and what follows from it, is seminal for the Hebrew scriptures. The tale of their ancestors' liberation from slavery is told and retold by Jews year on year, and points to two crucial aspects of God's character. Firstly, that God is compassionate and, secondly, that God works for justice: God knows about the suffering and is moved by it, and God will liberate the slaves.

This is what the Hebrew scriptures mean by 'justice': working to help those who are abused, oppressed or suffering. The Hebrew word is *tsedek*, which is sometimes translated into English as 'righteousness', although that is an unhelpful word as it means little to English speakers today and what it probably does suggest is not what is meant.[3] *Tsedek*, 'justice', is not a balancing of demands and entitlements but is about protecting the weak from the strong, supporting and assisting those who are disadvantaged, and setting free those who are controlled by others.

Mystery and Covenant

In the story Moses has lots of reasons why he does not want to go back to Egypt and become a leader, and one by one he comes out with his excuses. Like other Hebrew heroes, Moses too is human and this story, which is so important in the life of the people and their understanding of God, mixes humour with riddle. Before he embarks on his unsuccessful excuses, Moses says to God, 'When I go to the Israelites and tell them that God has sent me they will want to know your name.' And God replies: '*ehyeh ašer ehyeh*'.[4] This is profound, mysterious, and cryptic.

The phrase can be translated as 'I am who I am', or, because of the way that the Hebrew language works, 'I am what I am', or 'I will be who I will be', or 'I will be what I will be'. It seems to be connected with the name 'Yahweh', although quite how is not agreed. And it could be simply a way of refusing to answer the question. Yahweh is the God of Abraham, Isaac and Jacob, and will not be pinned down.[5]

They pass through the Sea of Reeds, or the Red Sea in more dramatic translations, and come to Mount Sinai. There Yahweh makes a covenant with them as God had with their ancestor Abraham. Yahweh will be their God and they will be God's people. To enable them to live as God's people, God instructs them how they are to live. God gives commandments which are the heart of the *Torah*: a word which has come to be used for the whole of the first five books of the Hebrew scriptures.

The Hebrew word *Torah* is often translated as 'Law', although *Torah* differs from the modern Western idea of law. *Torah* is a way of life, and a covenant is a relationship, not a contract. People and God are to be related to each other; not two impersonal entities in a binding agreement. The Torah points to how God's people are to behave within this covenant relationship.

A later summary by rabbis of the whole Torah was, 'Hear, O Israel: the Lord our God, the Lord is one; you shall love the Lord your God with all your heart, and with all your soul, and with all your strength. And you shall love your neighbour as yourself' (Deuteronomy 6.5 and Leviticus 19.18).[6] The people were not just to obey but to love God, and to do so with their whole being. In a contract you have to do what it says but you don't have to agree with it, or think about it, or even have any particular feelings for the other party. But a covenant is a binding relationship between two parties and, because the Hebrew understanding of the person was holistic, the covenant between God and the people must involve the whole person.

Commandments for life

Although the Torah was later summarised in two sentences, in the first five books of the Hebrew scriptures it runs into hundreds of instructions. These are now widely agreed to have built up over a period of time and to have finally been edited together during the Exile. But the core is the so-called Ten Commandments found in Exodus 20.1–17 and Deuteronomy 5.6–21.

The tenth forbids covetousness, which is the basis of consumerism. The ninth demands honesty. The eighth forbids theft. The seventh is about family relations and has also been interpreted as about property rights.[7] The sixth forbids murder. And the fifth calls for respect for parents.

The fourth commandment is about keeping the Sabbath as a holy day of rest for everyone, and everything. Slaves and foreigners, as well as domestic animals, were all to have one day in seven as a rest. Everyone was to have it together so they could worship God, study the Torah, and socialise. This was applied in an ancient agrarian economy but somehow seems to be beyond an industrial and economically strong society such as Britain.

The first three commandments are about God. The first is that the people should have no other gods except the One who released them from slavery.

The second is that they should not make any image or picture of God, let alone endow it with divine power. God remains ultimately mysterious and the people should not try to encapsulate or capture who or what God is in any way. The Hebrew scriptures do not speculate on what God is.

And the third commandment was to not make wrongful use of the name, or authority, of God. In due course, in order to avoid doing this by mistake, Jews stopped pronouncing the name of God, 'Yahweh', and when the name appeared in the scriptures they read it as 'Adonai', a word of respect for a lord or person of significance. Later they went further so that today the word is often simply read as 'The Name', meaning that the mystery of God's being is maintained. God is the One who creates, speaks, and gives life. God is not to be coerced, manipulated, or even finally understood. But God is to be trusted and the Commandments call for trust.

The Torah was intended to be life-enhancing.[8] In any community all sorts of suggestions emerge as to what should be done and how people should live. Some of these are simply ideas, although some may come with a claimed added weight because they were received in a vision, or a dream, or are said to come from a spirit or djinn. For the Israelites, or Jews, the Torah was a measure for such things. If suggestions ran counter to what the Torah said then they were not to be followed. God was the source of life and had given the Torah as a guide to living.

Questions in crisis

The question for the Jews in their exile in Babylon was whether God had reneged on the covenant, and whether it made any sense to worship and serve this God at all. The place where God was thought principally to be, the Holy Place in the Temple in Jerusalem, had been destroyed. The people were scattered from the land they thought God had given them. The old stories and songs told of Yahweh God going out with their armies as the 'Lord of Hosts' but they had now been utterly defeated. Was God also defeated?

Their reflections and heart-searching took them in various directions. No doubt there were some, possibly many, who saw Israel's loyalty to Yahweh as a mistake. New times call for new ways of living. These people would have assimilated into the Babylonian empire just as many of the people of the Northern Kingdom had done when that was destroyed by the Assyrians. But some reckoned there must be some other way of making sense of the situation.

One view was that God had not broken the covenant, but they had. There are two sides to a covenant and they reckoned they had failed to keep their side of it. The long narratives in the books of Joshua, Judges,

Samuel and Kings tell the tales. These are clearly a collection of oral histories made in a time of crisis so that the stories, and therefore the people's own identity, should not be lost. But they are also a long tale of the people failing to live as God had instructed them: bad kings had led the people into bad ways and so the failure of the covenant was their fault. It was the fault of the kings and of the people who followed them.

Words of condemnation and of hope

The books of the Prophets, collected together at this time, contained a similar theme. Micah, for example:

Can I tolerate wicked scales
  and a bag of dishonest weights?
Your wealthy are full of violence;
  your inhabitants speak lies,
  with tongues of deceit in their mouths.
Therefore I have begun to strike you down,
  making you desolate because of your sins. (Micah 6.11–14)

And Amos:

Take away from me the noise of your songs;
  I will not listen to the melody of your harps.
But let justice roll down like waters,
  and righteousness like an ever-flowing stream. (Amos 5.23–24)

Hosea struggled towards a conviction that God who had rescued Israel from slavery in Egypt would not give up on them.[9] Ezekiel looked towards a new Exodus, a return to the promised land, and a restoration of Jerusalem.[10] Some, like Isaiah, taught that all was not lost because Yahweh God was the creator of heaven and earth, and continued to care about the people in their Exile.

Thus says the Lord, your Redeemer,
  who formed you in the womb:
'I am the Lord, who made all things,
  who alone stretched out the heavens,
  who by myself spread out the earth; …

who says of Jerusalem, "It shall be rebuilt",
and of the temple, "Your foundation shall be laid."' (Isaiah 44.24, 28)

The wilderness and the dry land shall be glad,
the desert shall rejoice and blossom;
like the crocus it shall blossom abundantly,
and rejoice with joy and singing … (Isaiah 35.1–2)[11]

For all people

Such messages of hope had significant implications. One was that if God was not just the God of Israel, God must also be concerned with other tribes and peoples. This had been suggested by Amos, who condemned various tribes for their behaviour, even though they did not have the Torah which God had given to Israel.[12] Isaiah spoke about God using the pagan Persian ruler as God's anointed one, or 'messiah', to enable the Jews to return.[13]

Also, if God was with the chosen people even in their Exile, God could be worshipped in other places. So there developed the institution of the synagogue, a meeting house, in which prayers were said and the Torah studied. The Torah developed as a possible basis for a society loyal to Yahweh God in a very different place. When the Babylonian Empire was destroyed by the Persians and exiles were allowed to return to their homelands some Jews chose to go back to Palestine, although many chose not to and since that time most Jews have lived elsewhere.

It also followed that if God is concerned with all people, God must also be concerned *for* all people. The germ of this insight is there in the stories of Abraham when God says that through him 'all nations will be blessed'.[14] It is there in the concept of Israel being 'a priestly kingdom and a holy nation',[15] in that a priest exists within a society for the benefit of that society. Israel, the kingdom of priests, was to be that for other peoples.

And it is there in the Psalms:

The earth is the Lord's and all that is in it,
The world, and those who live in it.[16]

Some prophetic visions of a future reign of peace and justice were for all nations. There would be a time when God would 'judge between many peoples, and arbitrate between nations'.

'They shall beat their swords into ploughshares,
  and their spears into pruning-hooks;
nation shall not lift up sword against nation,
  neither shall they learn war any more;
but they shall all sit under their own vines and under their own fig trees,
  and no one shall make them afraid;
  for the mouth of the Lord of hosts has spoken.' (Micah 4.3–4)[17]

Wisdom writings

As well as the books of the Torah and the Prophets there are others simply referred to as the Writings. Some of these are specifically concerned with wisdom; principally with questions of how to live. However, Koheleth, the Preacher who wrote Ecclesiastes, indulged in speculation about the value of all his knowledge, and concluded that it was all empty air. There was a time and a place for everything. Better to live and enjoy the life you are given than struggle to accumulate wealth or wisdom.[18]

There is the interminable question of why bad things happen to good people. There are psalmists who do not seem to believe they do, but others who are clear this is the case and that somehow the powerful and wealthy get away with their wickedness. And using the device of a debate the book of Job tackles that issue head-on and gives the answer that the debaters are to stop arguing and to look at the Creation in awe.

Proverbs is mainly a collection of short, pithy, and easily remembered sayings to guide someone into living a good life. But the editor also speaks about Wisdom as a character who calls to the reader to attend to what she is saying:

'The Lord created me, Wisdom, at the beginning of his work,
  the first of his acts of long ago.

Ages ago I was set up,
  at the first, before the beginning of the earth …
  then I was beside him, like a master worker;
and I was daily his delight,
  rejoicing before him always,
rejoicing in his inhabited world
  and delighting in the human race …
Whoever finds me finds life
  and obtains favour from the Lord;
but those who miss me injure themselves;
  all who hate me love death.' (Proverbs 8:22–36)

To ignore the wisdom that is within the Creation is folly, and to hate it is deadly.

Flickering hope

Even after the return from exile hope remained an issue for Jews. The Temple was rebuilt but it was a shadow of its alleged former glory. After the Persians came the Greeks who began bloody culture wars and sometimes persecuted Jews who kept to their old ways. People looked back to a glorious past and the ways that God had rescued and supported their ancestors. They looked at their present oppression and persecution and some took up arms to fight for the freedom to worship the One God as they had been taught. They looked ahead for better times, or a new age when God would reign and the arrogant and brutal emperors would be overthrown.

Even when the more pragmatic Romans took over from the Greeks life for Jews was still far from satisfactory and they hoped for God to act decisively in history. Some thought God would bring liberation through a military leader or a powerful teacher of righteousness. Others thought that a superhuman or angelic figure would break through into the world from the realm of God. In the Roman province of Palestine in the first century there were a number of preachers, prophets or wannabe leaders who caused agitation among the Jews. Among them was Jesus of Nazareth, whom we now need to consider.

Chapter 10

Jesus and the reign of God:
Matthew, Mark, Luke

There was a time not many decades ago when some theologians were sceptical about knowing anything about the man, Jesus of Nazareth. The problem is that the principal source for knowing about Jesus is the books of the New Testament, and particularly the four gospels. They differ and they are not the kind of 'Life and Times of Jesus' that many readers would like to have available. They do not claim to be biographies in the modern sense but messages of good news, or *godspel* in Old English. Each of the writers conveyed their message in their own way with their own emphasis, which was in part affected by the concerns of the group of people they were writing for.

There were many Christians for whom this was not a problem. They would study the books because they believed them to be somehow written or inspired by God, or because they were the received holy books of the church to which they belonged, or because they had a message about the world which made sense to them. The Christian movement did not grind to a halt because of the scepticism of some theologians.[1]

However, these reasons for carrying on had their own problems. The gospels claim to be about a person who lived and did things. If the gospels simply become a story, albeit 'the greatest story ever told', they might remain powerful but are no more a source of hope than any other very good story.[2] The gospels might inspire and present a blueprint for radical political action, or be a guide for an ascetic spiritual path, or help in the mental healing of individuals, or encourage groups in their struggles for justice, but questions remain. Why these books in particular? Is there any reason for believing that we shall overcome the powers that oppress us, as these books seem to suggest? Is there any basis for accepting them as a guide for living? How do we deal with the inconsistencies? What do we do about the bits which are unbelievable or downright nasty?[3] Such questions bubble up to the surface from time to time.

The man behind the myth

It is now clear that behind the gospels was a man, Jesus of Nazareth. As the Jewish scholar Geza Vermes put it: 'There was a real Jesus, without any doubt. Over the space of months, or perhaps two or three years, this Jesus of flesh and blood was seen and heard around the countryside of Galilee and in Jerusalem, an uncompromising, single-minded lover of God and his fellow-beings, convinced that by his example and by his teaching he could infect them with his own passionate sense of relation with the Father in heaven. And he did so.'[4]

In the last few decades more documents from the first century have been discovered, there has been closer study of Jewish rabbinic literature from the period around the time of Jesus and of writings from the early decades of the Christian movement, and deeper study of the social history of the time with the application of social scientific methods and models to the documents. An enormous amount has been done to give a bigger picture of the man behind the gospels. They do not provide the detail: what he did when, and so on. But they do help us see in a better light what was going on.

According to Vermes, Jesus was a Holy Man, in the spirit of the prophets Elijah and Elisha, and was by no means the only one to emerge in Galilee in the first decades of the first century. He was, like others, a teacher, preacher, healer and exorcist. Jesus clearly knew the Hebrew scriptures well, and Vermes reckons that he taught obedience to the Torah not just in the letter, but in the spirit. That is certainly what Matthew's Gospel seems to suggest.[5]

The gospels themselves are like windows through which we can look into a room. Because they were written with different readerships in mind, and by different people who themselves belonged to different groups within the Christian movement, we see Jesus from different angles. The wider research helps us interpret what we are seeing. The differences between the gospels are not a problem but can be an asset if we want to know not so much what exactly happened but what Jesus' life might mean for people.

Several gospels

There are, of course, four gospels included in the New Testament. Three of them, Matthew, Mark and Luke, usually referred to as the 'synoptic gospels', are similar while John is different in style and content.[6] Also relevant are the letters of St Paul, which were probably written before the earliest of the gospels.

The gospels and letters were all written within a generation or two of Jesus' work in Galilee. How reliable are they? The writers did not have the notebooks, cameras and recorders that we have now but, on the other hand, because of this they relied more on their memories and so were better at remembering. The writers were probably not eyewitnesses to much, or even any, of what happened and the stories and sayings of Jesus were used in preaching and teaching and so got adapted over time.

So, though while reading the gospels we can imagine the situations or encounters being described, what we have in our minds is not what our smartphone would have captured if we had been around at the time. But neither are we dealing with pure fiction: behind the gospels lie historical events and the person of Jesus. In most cases it is not possible to sift out what actually happened and we are reliant on what the first followers of Jesus said about him. We look at Jesus through the lenses of the gospels.[7]

We will focus on the synoptic gospels because they contain the basic stories and sayings of Jesus: what Jesus did and what he taught. John's Gospel includes long speeches purportedly by Jesus but they are largely a stage removed from the parables and sayings of the man we see in the synoptics. The long speeches in John can be understood as reflections on who Jesus was and what his life meant. Similarly, references to Jesus in the other early Christian writings are largely theological reflections about him.

In all three synoptic gospels there are several recurrent themes: three of which are the Fatherhood of God, the grace of God, and the reign of God. They are interconnected and all relate to the question of hope.

The Fatherhood of God

Jesus was a man of his time and it was a patriarchal society. Despite the long and beautiful tradition of the Jewish mother who loves her sons, the father was the head of the family. For Jesus, as for earlier Hebrew writers, God was Father *par excellence*. Not a domineering or demanding father, let alone a brutal or bullying father, but a father who loves his children. This was not new. It was a theme of the prophet Hosea.[8] It is found in Proverbs, and the Psalms.[9] So it is that in Matthew Jesus teaches his disciples to pray, 'Our Father in heaven,' and repeatedly refers to God as 'your Father', or 'my Father'.[10]

After two thousand years in which this metaphor has been repeatedly used to bolster male dominance, and as some people's experience of their own father is less than good, we can find this hard. But when we look at Jesus' teaching we also find him telling a parable about a woman kneading dough. Immediately after the famous story of the shepherd who looks for a lost sheep, there is another story of a woman who searches for and finds a lost coin.[11] Jesus taught women, which was contrary to the practice of the time,[12] he had women among his followers,[13] he was known to associate with prostitutes, and made one into an exemplar of faith in a confrontation with a Pharisee who had criticised her and him.[14]

If Christians think they are stuck with the images their church has used in the past, then they have to carry on talking about God being male. But if they see Jesus as initiating a movement and setting courses for the future, then they have great scope for developing images, retrieving neglected ones from the Bible, and creating new metaphors. It is not uncommon now for the Lord's Prayer to be begun, 'Loving God in heaven …'[15] From New Zealand there is a version which begins:

Eternal Spirit, Earth-maker, Pain-bearer, Life-giver,
Source of all that is and that shall be,
Father and Mother of us all,
Loving God, in whom is heaven …[16]

The grace of God

The theme of the grace of God fits closely with the image of God as a loving parent. The classic parable of this is Jesus' story of two brothers, often in the past known as The Prodigal Son.[17] Jesus spoke on many occasions about God's love and forgiveness. He also lived it, and had a reputation of being a friend of 'sinners'. In response to criticism for this, Jesus said, 'It is not the well who need a doctor but the sick' (Mark 2.17).

This theme is not original to Jesus. Jesus quotes the prophet Hosea, saying to his Pharisee critics, 'Go and learn what this means: "I desire mercy not sacrifice."'[18] And as we have seen, back in the founding stories of Israel in the book of Exodus, God hears the cries of the Hebrew slaves and comes to rescue them. Later, in the prophetic writings, God promises to act to save the Israelites in their oppression and exile.[19] This connects with our third theme: the reign of God.

The reign of God

Both Matthew and Mark have Jesus begin his work in Galilee proclaiming, 'The time is fulfilled, and the kingdom of God has come near; repent, and believe in the good news' (Matthew 4.17, Mark 1.15).

The original Greek text is notoriously difficult to translate. What 'The time is fulfilled' means is not obvious. 'Come near' is even harder because it could mean about to come, or already present. While the phrase 'The kingdom' of God, *basilea* in Greek, or *malkut* in Hebrew, suffers from being well known and frequently misunderstood. The 'kingdom' is not a place, it is a reign. And the phrase points to it being God who does, or who will, reign. The supreme power is God's, and God will exercise it.

This was a message of hope to people who desperately needed it. Life for the Galilean peasants to whom Jesus preached was hard. Poverty was intense. A few people owned a great deal while most owned little or nothing, or were in debt. Life was about getting by from day to day and keeping your head down because you had no agency: no power to change things. Power was with the political and economic elite, and ultimately with the distant Roman Emperor who exercised his authority through the ever-present army. There were puppet kings like Herod, and a Council in Jerusalem, who were themselves wealthy and oppressive, but Rome ruled. A message that God's reign was beginning would be good news. But what did it mean?

Jesus did not invent the phrase. It goes back to the early days of settled Israel when their God, Yahweh, was king.[20] Even when there was a glorification of the kingship of David and his successors, or when a future liberator would be 'a king in the line of David',[21] there remained a tradition that when the people had first wanted a king it was a betrayal of Yahweh's kingship.[22]

Interestingly, in the gospels Jesus never speaks of God as king.[23] He comes close to it in a couple of parables in Matthew's gospel, which in Luke are about 'a rich man'. But these are only ways of speaking about God if the parable is treated as an allegory. Otherwise, God is 'Father'.

However, Jesus spoke frequently of the 'reign of God',[24] which could be understood in a number of ways:

(i) A transcendent realm which people may look to for inspiration but which they will only enter at death or in a great cataclysmic judgement. This is a way of thinking that came to the fore two centuries before Jesus when the Jews were being oppressed and persecuted by their Greek rulers. A whole genre of literature developed with alleged visions of what the future judgement would mean: the so-called apocalyptic literature.[25]

(ii) Transcendent now but coming into the world in the future, forming a new social order. Matthew 6.10, in the Lord's Prayer, can be seen this way: 'Your kingdom come, your will be done on earth as it is in heaven.' Mark 10.35 onwards envisages a new order, as do some of Jesus' words about rewards,[26] and his words at the Last Supper in Luke 22.28–30.

(iii) A special hidden realm which exists within society and influences the whole. Jesus' parables about yeast and about mustard seed suggest this.[27]

(iv) Present now in the work of Jesus. 'If it is by the Spirit of God that I cast out demons,' says Jesus, 'then know that the reign of God has come upon you'(Matthew 12.28).[28] And when John the Baptist's disciples come to him and ask if he is 'the one who is to come', Jesus tells them to look at what is going on around him, and depicts a fulfilment of Isaiah's prophecy of the reign of God.[29]

(v) Among people now, like a plant growing or yeast raising dough.[30] In Luke 17.20 Jesus says, 'The kingdom of God is not coming with things that can be observed; nor will they say, "Look, here it is!" or "There it is!" For, in fact, the kingdom of God is among you.' Or within you.[31]

Things are complicated further by Jesus' frequent references to an enigmatic figure, 'the Son of Man'. This references a heavenly figure 'like a son of man' coming to deliver the world in the book of Daniel.[32] But it could simply be a human person, as when Ezekiel is addressed in his vision of a valley of dry bones.[33] Jesus refers to the coming of the Son of Man as if it is a future event but also seems to use the phrase to refer to himself.[34]

What did it mean?

What did Jesus mean by his talk of the reign of God? How did the gospel writers understand it? And how did Jesus' hearers understand it?

New Testament scholar Ed Sanders reckoned that Jesus of Nazareth could have held all these ideas. 'There is no difficulty in thinking that Jesus thought the kingdom was in heaven, that people would enter it in the future, and that it was also present in some of his own work.' (E.P. Sanders, *The Historical Figure of Jesus*, p.178)[35] Or, we might add, present in those who accepted his message and trusted in God.

The synoptic gospel writers have different emphases, but none of them excludes any of these possible ideas. Matthew sees Jesus as a new Moses creating within Israel a new people of God who will bring reform to the whole. While he has a long passage which looks towards a day of judgement, he has another which consists of instructions as to how the new community is to behave.[36] Luke wrote two volumes, his Gospel and the Acts of the Apostles, and clearly has his eye on Jesus being a 'light to lighten the Gentiles'.[37] Mark's Gospel is brief and action-packed but, like the others, includes all possible understandings within his text.

But what did Jesus' hearers think if Jesus said all these things? One theme running through the gospels is that people misunderstand Jesus. They hear what they want to hear. Even Jesus' closest disciples fail to understand what he is saying and doing, and they have extra tuition. However, there is little doubt that people saw Jesus as a prophet, they experienced him as a healer and exorcist, they heard him as a compelling speaker who taught authoritatively and as someone who was willing to challenge the traditionalists when he thought they had it wrong. It also seems that when Jesus went to Jerusalem many of the people expected great things.

And now?

Within the last century or so Jesus has been seen as an apocalyptic prophet who expected the cataclysmic Day of Judgement in his own time, and was mistaken.[38] Or as an ethical teacher.[39] Or as a revolutionary who was challenging the imperial power structures and creating a new community.[40] Or as one in whose actions the reign of God was present, and in whose successive disciples it is still present.[41] Jesus has also been seen as someone who challenged people to decide here and now for the sake of God and for their own authentic living.[42] All of these interpretations have their strengths but, as Sanders points out, have their weaknesses too, and involve leaving something out.[43]

For example, if we are to believe Jesus was simply announcing the imminent Day of Judgement, we have to explain why he taught people in a way that envisaged a continuing alternative community. Or, if the reign of God is only now, why does so much happen in the world which is contrary to what a ruling parent God would tolerate? And if Jesus was working for revolution and his disciples were to follow his example, what would happen after the revolution had come?

Jesus' preaching about the reign of God was heard as a message of hope by his Galilean hearers. We will consider later whether it might also be a message of hope for a wider audience, including ourselves, but first we need to think not only about what Jesus said and did, but also about what happened to him. Because that threw his whole message of the reign of God into doubt, and also opened up new possibilities about its significance.

Chapter 11

What happened to Jesus:
Matthew, Mark, Luke, Acts

The scribes and Pharisees are the Bad Guys in the synoptic gospels, even though Jesus actually had a lot in common with them. The scribes were an occupational group. Scribes had originally been the people who copied the scriptures but became in time the experts at knowing what was in them and how they should be interpreted. Basically, they were lawyers.

The Pharisees were a sort of religious political party but, having said that, as there was no democracy the idea of a political party is an anachronism, and in Hebrew or Jewish thinking of the time there was no separation of religion and politics.[1] The idea of a separation emerged in Europe following the seventeenth-century wars of religion and with the Enlightenment.

Divisions and differences

In Jesus' divided society the disparity between a super-rich elite and the mass of landless peasants was enormous. Taxes were raised by a system of tax-farming in which someone had a contract to raise a certain amount of money from an area and went out to get it with the help of the army. The army was everywhere and was the visible manifestation of the dreadful power of Rome. Armies marched with their standards decorated with pagan symbols, and the currency was Roman coinage stamped with the head of the Emperor and more pagan symbols. It all oozed idolatry and was an abomination to pious and poor Jewish peasants.

There was a small 'middle class' of skilled workers, which would include stonemasons and possibly a *tekton*, or carpenter-builder, like Jesus. Fishing might also be a small business, so it could be that Simon and his colleagues belonged to that class. That did not mean they were comfortably off. The possibility of a shortage of work or a poor catch was always present and could lead to hunger and debt. Pharisees largely came from this class. They were sticklers for keeping the Torah and its developments over the years, although to do that you needed be above the breadline.

According to Matthew, Jesus was also concerned that the Law be kept. However, he disagreed with the Pharisees about how it was to be interpreted and its detailed application, and he raised the bar as far as righteousness was concerned. For Jesus it was not the externals that mattered but a person's attitude. Good fruit comes from good trees.[2]

He also disagreed with the Pharisees about the attitude of God. To the Pharisees the Torah was a gift from God,[3] so living as God required was only possible because of God's grace, or gift. Jesus wanted that attitude to be applied to all relationships, so, while the Pharisees would want to keep themselves apart from people they thought might be a bad influence, Jesus mixed with sinners and told them about the love and forgiveness of God. Early in the synoptic gospels the scribes and Pharisees want to get rid of Jesus. Later he turns on them and criticises them in no uncertain terms.[4]

Jesus agreed with the Pharisees about resurrection. This idea, or belief, came, perhaps from Persia, into Jewish thinking two or three centuries before Jesus. The Hebrew scriptures are vague about or uninterested in any kind of afterlife. What mattered was that one's family line should continue.[5] But during the persecutions two centuries before Jesus the question arose of what justice there could be for martyrs who had died because of their allegiance to the God of Israel. The answer was that there would be a day when the dead would be raised to new life, the faithful would be honoured and the unfaithful would have everlasting contempt.[6]

Daniel, which was one of the latest writings to be included in the Hebrew canon of scripture, includes this idea. Earlier writings contained hints of a resurrection idea, but these could also be metaphors for the restoration of Israel.[7] In Job, another late book, the suffering man declares that he knows that his redeemer lives and that he shall see him 'in the flesh' on the last day.[8]

When Jesus began preaching around Galilee that the reign of God was at hand it would have caused expectations of this great day when the dead would be raised. Jesus was not the first such preacher and neither was he the last. Galilee was a hotbed of apocalyptic thinking and possible revolt.[9]

Jerusalem

Sadducees come into the story when Jesus goes to Jerusalem. Sadducees were a kind of religious aristocracy: priestly families who, unlike British aristocrats with their country seats, had their homes near the Temple in Jerusalem.[10] They were religious conservatives and, whereas Pharisees would happily study the Prophets and the wisdom writings, for the Sadducees the only true scripture was the Torah. They had no time for recent ideas like resurrection.

Also in Jerusalem were supporters or hangers-on of the Herod family who had held power in Palestine for several generations, were mistrusted and hated by the peasants and were only kept in position by the Romans. There was a continual balancing act going on. It was often easier for the Roman government if, in marginal areas like Palestine, they could rule indirectly through local kings and aristocrats like the Herods, but sometimes these locals were unable to control the populace and Rome would put in a Governor to rule directly, as in Judea at the time of Jesus. Herodians and Sadducees operated under Rome's umbrella. They would have seen it as realpolitik. Rome was invincible and Rome also brought order. It was a system that suited those with wealth and power, as long as they played their cards right. And one of the keys was to keep control.

Jesus had other ideas. He taught that leadership was about service. According to Luke he said to his disciples, 'The kings of the Gentiles lord it over them; and those in authority over them are called benefactors. But not so with you; rather the greatest among you must become like the youngest, and the leader like one who serves' (Luke 22.25).

Having control of the Temple gave the priests considerable power, which they abused. They demanded a particular coinage for use in the Temple collections, ostensibly to avoid having pagan images, and demanded that animals for sacrifice were up to standard. They then fixed the exchange rate for coins and the prices of certified animals. When Jesus arrived in Jerusalem he staged a demonstration, a symbolic prophetic act, and cleared out the moneychangers and animal sellers.[11]

According to Matthew and Luke, the Pharisees and Sadducees then challenged Jesus with two questions. One about whether it was lawful to pay taxes to Rome, and the other about resurrection. About taxation Jesus said, 'Give to the Emperor what belongs to the Emperor and to God what belongs to God' (Matthew 22.21). A brilliant and enigmatic response which people have been arguing about ever since. About resurrection he said that the God of Abraham, Isaac and Jacob is not God of the dead but of the living. This cleverly referred to a part of the scriptures which the Sadducees accepted as authoritative. And it also suggests that Jesus conceived of resurrection as a present reality.[12]

Rebels

There were other Jewish groups in the social mix of Palestine at the time of Jesus. Down by the Dead Sea were Essenes: a quasi-monastic group who followed a historical or mythological figure called the Teacher of Righteousness, and who aimed to purify themselves to take part in a great war against the pagans that would come at the End Time. Out and about in the hills were groups of bandits who carried out robberies and violent attacks against Rome and its super-rich lackeys.

There were some among the bandits and other people among the general population who wanted an armed insurrection against Rome. They would have been inspired by the stories of the Maccabees' earlier struggle against the Syrian Greeks,[13] and also, no doubt, by apocalyptic writings or speeches about the forthcoming reign of God. In the gospel lists of Jesus' disciples is one called Simon the Zealot, who may have had such hopes.[14]

When Jesus went around preaching in rural Galilee he seems not to have had a political programme, but he did have very different values from the political wheeler-dealers in Jerusalem. To him the great power was not Rome but God. It was from God that people must take their bearings and in so doing they must not just love neighbours but also enemies, and that would have included the Romans. They were not to take up arms but practise what has later come to be called creative non-violence.[15] They must lend without expecting any return, and forgive those who harmed them.[16] It sounds gentle and meek but it was actually undermining the status quo. And to the powermongers in Jerusalem, whether or not they picked up what he was actually doing and saying, there was the fact that he came from Galilee, which they saw as a hotbed of rebellion, and he had a large following, so Jesus was a threat.

Confrontation

As is well known, Jesus chose to come into Jerusalem at a festival time when there were massive crowds in a fever of excitement, and to do so on a donkey. This fitted with a prophecy about a king coming in peace[17] and everyone would have recognised that. He enacted a purification of the Temple and disputed with the scribes, Pharisees and Sadducees in the Temple courtyards. After several days of this, on the Thursday night, he had a meal with his closest disciples, and was later arrested. There was some sort of show trial, and he was handed over to the Roman Governor, Pontius Pilate, who eventually ordered him to be flogged and crucified.

There is much speculation about what Jesus expected to happen: whether he thought God would intervene cataclysmically, whether he expected the rulers to acknowledge their fault and adopt his teaching about ruling in accord with the values and ways of God, or whether he expected to be killed. There are occasions in the gospels when Jesus warns his disciples that he must suffer and die, but these could have been written into the story with hindsight. What we know happened, is that he was crucified.

Crucifixion was, of course, a painful way to die: literally, excruciating. But the New Testament writers say little about the pain involved. That is a later European concern. Nor do they give details about how it was done. There were many ways of crucifying someone. Crucifixion was the Romans' standard method for dealing with rebels and the particular method probably depended on what materials and time were available.

What the New Testament writers emphasise more is the shame of the cross. 'Cursed is every man who hangs on a tree', says the Torah.[18] In this very hierarchical society a crucified man was below the lowest of the low. He was rubbish.

The men among Jesus' disciples ran away, which was unheroic but reasonable. There was nothing they could do and they could be next. Some women stayed nearby. But for all of them this must have been a time of despair, as it may have been for Jesus himself. In both Mark and Matthew Jesus cries out as he dies, 'My God, my God, why have you forsaken me?'[19] It is a quote from a psalm but it is also the words of a despairing man. In Luke, Jesus prays that his executioners would be forgiven, and he tells a criminal dying beside him that he will be with him that day in Paradise.[20] We are told that Jesus died after six hours or so on the cross and was buried nearby in a tomb provided by one of the aristocrats.[21]

After crucifixion

The synoptic gospel accounts of Jesus' work and death are remarkably down to earth. At the beginning of Matthew and Luke we have birth narratives which are different in each case but include angels, a moving star, and shepherds seeing a heavenly chorus. But once Jesus comes into Galilee announcing the reign of God there are no angels. Yes, he provides a miraculous meal for a big crowd and walks on water, he is seen transfigured by three of his closest disciples, and he heals people and casts out demons. But, bearing in mind that there had been thirty years of storytelling and preaching in which the stories about Jesus could have been elaborated, what the gospels say remains pretty low key. And Jesus' trial and crucifixion are told in a very matter-of-fact way.

Then we move into a different mode. According to the gospels, Jesus was 'raised from the dead', and it is impossible to pin down exactly what that means as some kind of event. But there are three things which are known historically to have happened and which bear on the statement that Jesus was 'raised'. The first is that after a short period of time Jesus' disciples were in Jerusalem preaching that he had been raised, and the movement that Jesus had begun grew and developed. This was despite the opposition of the Jewish and Roman authorities with their threats, floggings and executions.

The second is that this announcement was supported by claims that Jesus had appeared to some of the disciples. The descriptions they give are of something unique and very strange. The raised man can allegedly be touched and eats with them, but is able to appear in a locked room. And when they see him, he does not appear to be anyone other than an ordinary man.[22]

The third thing is that the tomb of Jesus was said to be empty and it would have been easy for the authorities at the time to prove otherwise, but they did not. If the authorities had taken the body they would have produced it. If Jesus' disciples had taken the body someone would have said so, once the persecutions and torture began.

David Jenkins, former Bishop of Durham, allegedly said, 'A conjuring trick with bones is not the Resurrection.' His point was that the Christian message about the Resurrection was not fundamentally about an empty tomb, and neither was it dependent on it.[23] The disciples did not preach an empty tomb. They preached that Jesus had risen. And in the four different gospels they told about it in similar but also rather different ways.

In Mark the women go to the tomb but find it empty. A young man in white tells them that Jesus is risen and they are to tell Peter and the disciples that he will go before them into Galilee where they will see him. Back to Galilee. Back to the beginning of the gospel, to start again, but this time with themselves as the actors.[24]

In Matthew an earthquake and an angel move the stone away from the tomb, and Jesus meets the women when they go there. He then meets with the disciples in Galilee and tells them to go to 'all nations', to baptise them and to teach people to obey his teaching. Jesus, who had previously restricted his mission to Jews, now tells his followers to go worldwide, with the promise that he would be with them 'till the end of the age'.[25]

Luke's Gospel has a sequel, the Acts of the Apostles, which tells of the Christian movement spreading through the Eastern Mediterranean region. His gospel ends with Jesus meeting with his disciples, 'withdrawing from them' and being 'carried up into heaven', which is where the angels came from at the beginning of the gospel. 'Heaven' is the realm of God. The Greek word is variously translated as heaven or as sky.[26] Luke continues the story in his second book with the Holy Spirit coming from heaven, or the wind coming out of the sky, onto the disciples and equipping them for their mission.[27]

Before this drama Luke tells a story of two despondent disciples walking from Jerusalem a couple of days after Jesus' crucifixion and meeting up with a stranger.[28] On the journey he explains to them how the Messiah had to suffer in order to 'enter into his glory', 'as Moses and the Prophets had said'. Ever since Luke wrote it Christians have wondered exactly which parts of Moses and the Prophets he might have been thinking of. The servant songs in Isaiah are an obvious possibility,[29] as is the Exodus story, reinterpreted. The suffering of Jeremiah, perhaps. Or the whole Exile experience of Israel, with the death of the nation and its being resurrected as a renewed people of God both in Judea and Galilee and in the diaspora. But in the story the disciples do not recognise the stranger as Jesus until they sit down for a meal and the stranger breaks the bread in a familiar way: a description that echoes the ritual meals of the first Christian communities.[30]

And now?

We are concerned with whether there is any reasonable basis for hope now in the face of the ecological crisis and other threats to our existence. We have looked at the ancient writings because they might help. There are clearly in the Hebrew and Christian scriptures many wise sayings and intriguing stories but they come from a time when people understood the world very differently. While we can use our imaginations to explore and reflect on what they are saying, for them to be anything more than entertainment or moral exhortations we need to be able to interpret them into our own way of understanding the world.

There is talk in some Christian circles about a 'biblical world view', but there was no one world view. The views and insights of Egyptians, Babylonians, Persians and Greeks all influenced the writers' understandings of the world. The view of an educated Jewish trader who travelled the Eastern Mediterranean at the time of Jesus would have been very different from that of a Galilean or Judean peasant scratching a living as a day labourer or a fisherman. People's ways of seeing the world differed and were in a continual state of flux.

Nevertheless, all the ways that the writers of these ancient texts saw the world would have been very different from how we understand it now. To them the world was vast, but nothing like as vast as the size of the earth as we can now measure it, and that in turn is tiny in comparison with the scale of the solar system, let alone our galaxy. Most people then would have thought of the earth as more or less flat, perhaps with a dome of sky, and so on. There is a gulf between how they thought about the world and what might happen in it and the way we currently understand the cosmos and the nature of life on earth.

However, they did not hear or read their scriptures principally as giving them information about the nature of the world, but as poetry, stories and songs about life, and about God. Whether the Red Sea really parted to let the freeing slaves escape the Egyptians, or whether Elijah was really taken up to heaven in a chariot, was not an issue. What was at issue was what God was like, what mattered to God, and how they were to live day by day.

They were also concerned about hope. Whether there was any hope for them, their families and their tribe. For them, if God was to rescue them from oppressive rulers, save them from desperate poverty, give them food, and rebuild the community, God had to engage with the world and not just have sympathy with them or issue them with instructions. And they clearly believed that God did.

To see whether these scriptures have any relevance to us with our concern about hope we need to see whether we can interpret some of what they say about God into our own way of understanding the cosmos, life, and society.

Part 4

THEOLOGY

Chapter 12

Talking about God:
Problems and possibilities

Before I start I need to make two declarations. One is a declaration of interest and the other is of trepidation. I am going to try to interpret into our present-day way of thinking about the world what I have suggested the Hebrew and Christian scriptures say which is relevant to the question of hope. But the first thing I need to say is that I am not coming to this cold. As I said in chapter 6, out of all the available sources of ancient wisdom, one of the reasons I have deliberately chosen these is because I am familiar with them and have spent many years as a member of the Christian church. The second thing I need to say is that some parts of the Bible are awful. There are passages which I, like many other people, find morally repugnant either because of what is said or because of what is simply taken for granted. We need to address both these issues before going any further.

Personal involvement

Even in scientific work a person looking for understanding is personally involved in the process. They have assumptions, background knowledge, their own history, commitments, and often a vested interest in the results.[1] That is unavoidable and it is one of the reasons that peer review is so important. It means people with similar skills but a different investment can consider the arguments and conclusions and check them out. And as a result they can between them develop a more robust understanding.

Personal involvement is even more pronounced in any investigation where belief and commitment are aspects of the actual subject being considered. Questions about life, faith and hope are going to be particularly demanding. We come to the questions with our prior set of ideas and then subject them to examination. But these are *our* ideas: *our* beliefs. They may be ways of seeing things which have shaped our life up till this point, and now we are questioning them. That is neither easy nor comfortable.

The question of hope is a big one. It is about our lives: our future. But more than that, it is about everyone we know and the life of the planet we live on. It cannot get much bigger than that, and it is hard to be coolly objective when we are so involved. But if our hope is to be anything more than bravado we need to assess what we think and not just blunder blindly on.

Texts of hope and terror

In the previous section I outlined a few of the themes in the Hebrew and Christian scriptures which I think are relevant to the question of hope. There are many other themes in these ancient texts which I have chosen to ignore because I am trying to address one pressing question and to see if these scriptures can help us.

I am not making any claims about their authority, although I have in the past belonged to churches which made quite extravagant claims about the origins and authority of the Bible. In some Christian groups there is even an idea that everything contained within the Bible is of equal merit and importance. This is not a view that has been held by the historic Churches or within Judaism. For Jews, the Torah is of supreme importance and probably most Christian churches value the gospels more highly than the other books. Anyone who does want to argue that the whole Bible is authoritative has to recognise that those scriptures also contain some pretty unpleasant material.

People can go to church regularly for years and not realise that what is read there, or recommended for personal reading, leaves out many of the nasty bits. But wars, massacres, violence against women, and racism are all there. There is also an assumed patriarchy, an acceptance of slavery, and condemnations of homosexuality.[2]

Some of it is literary device, like in a sci-fi novel or computer game where there are goodies and baddies, and we see this in the stories of the conquest of Canaan or Samson killing Philistines.[3] Some is a matter of interpretation, as with the concept of 'dominion' which we have already considered. Some is simply an acceptance of the widespread

Middle Eastern institutions of the time, like patriarchy, prostitution, and slavery. But some is not.

These books are my theological roots and there are things in them which I find objectionable, simply wrong, or even abhorrent. But having said that, I can also give a few reasons for not completely writing off this collection of ancient scriptures, and I hope that the chapters which follow will bear that out.

Joining a debate

These scriptures are a library of books written over a period of time and some ideas and assumptions changed in that period. As I said in chapter 6, in engaging with these books we are witnessing and taking part in a debate. We can read, critique and think about them. They were not written by God with every part to be taken as a directive for all time but were stories, poems, commandments, proverbs, songs, and more, written initially for their time but now available to us. We cannot expect everything they say to have relevance to us, and we are free to question them. We may sometimes find that in criticising or questioning the texts, new wisdom or encouragement is forthcoming.

In the Christian scriptures we find Jesus repeatedly reinterpreting the Torah and challenging accepted views of his time: for example, in the way he had women among his group of disciples, held up non-Jews as exemplars of faith in God, and taught love for enemies and active non-violence.[4]

It probably also needs to be said that while twenty-first-century readers might be horrified by some of the attitudes among the writers of the Hebrew scriptures, people of that time and culture would be horrified at some of our culture's general attitudes and behaviour. They would be shocked by our lack of hospitality to people in need, such as asylum seekers; by our society's callous disregard for the welfare of future generations in what we are doing to the climate; by our impersonal social relationships; and by the weapons of mass destruction which are simply accepted by many people and even endorsed by some Christians and Jews.

Interpreting the myths

We thought in chapter 6 about how the scriptures contain many kinds of literature, including myths in the opening chapters of Genesis. That raises a question as to what extent any talk of God is mythological. Like fantasy, myths take place in an imaginary world, but the question of hope is about our real world and anything we draw from these scriptures has to engage with the world as we know it. It is no use if all thought of God is restricted to a fantasy world: a Bible Land in which seas part to help the Israelites escape, the sun stops in the sky to enable them to continue slaughtering their enemies, and a star moves across the sky to lead wise men to a baby in a stable.

But we also noted that while in modern English usage the word ‘myth’ has come to mean something that is widely believed but not true, in its more technical sense ‘myth’ is a very useful concept. In religious studies and anthropology the word ‘myth’ is used to describe a way of interpreting experience. It is one among a number of ways of understanding or interpreting the world and of communicating insight. Different fields of knowledge use a variety of ways of doing this. Physics is very dependent on mathematical symbols and methods, but it also uses images, metaphors and theoretical models. Other fields of study rely more on words and grammar, or case studies, pictures, music, diagrams, graphs, proverbs, or allusions. Different tools are used for different jobs.

As it is understood anthropologically, myth provides meaning for experiences and gives value to life. It links different aspects of social life together, and is often more than a story but something that is acted out, sung or danced, as in the Jewish Passover meal or in the Christian Communion service and in baptism. So, a lot of talk about God is mythological in the sense that it takes the form of a significant story in which God is a character. It is also mythological in the sense that the stories interpret people’s experiences of life and the world.

If talk of ‘God’ were restricted to the myths of the opening chapters of Genesis it would make sense to consider God as simply a character in a powerful and useful but ultimately fictional tale. God would be like the elves of Middle-earth or the witches of Discworld. But ‘God’ continues to be spoken of in the Hebrew and Christian scriptures and is throughout them the subject of legends, poems, proverbs, prophecies, letters and other types of literature. Talk about God is not restricted to the myths but is fundamental to most of the ancient Hebrew and Christian writings of whatever sort, and to Christian and Jewish thinking as it has developed.

God and reality

We could put the question another way and ask how 'real' God is, but that obviously depends on what we mean by 'real'. If only what can be measured or analysed is real, then God is not real, but neither are many things that make life worth living, such as humour, friendship and love.

In most, if not all, fields of enquiry we hold that our theories correspond to some extent with something that is real. They are not just mental constructs. And if we are an inquisitive person or society we continue to critique our ideas and amend them to make them better fit what we experience of reality.

Most of us operate that way without analysing it. We work on the basis that much of what we think relates to a world 'out there'. We reckon that our ideas about cats and dogs, other people, roads and railways, electricity, atoms, geometric progressions, chord sequences, and GDP, although they might be a bit vague or in a process of change, are still about a real world. They are mental constructs which help us make sense of, or influence, what is real.

When we think, we do so in many different ways, using our imagination and our capacity for abstract thought. Our abstractions are powerful tools which help us individuals cope with and affect our part of the world, and as a society they enable us to achieve great things. Our technology is both marvellous and terrifying. With various intellectual tools we can also reflect on our relationships with other people, and with the cosmos and the Transcendent.

Our ideas can, of course, also distract us from the real world. We can spend too much time in our heads, or we can think our ideas are reality. It is worth pondering how many people have returned from a war and found that the country they had been fighting for was not actually what they had thought it was.[5]

We will proceed on the basis that while we use stories and metaphors in talking about the transcendent reality we call 'God', the stories and metaphors point towards something real. It is not something that can be measured or defined, but neither is it simply imaginary. None of our ideas or images is adequate for the task, which is why the scriptures have so many images and why we keep revising our thinking and developing new ones. But the work of theology is not simply a mind game, it is about what is real.[6]

He, She or It?

There is one other preliminary issue we need to consider, and that is whether it is appropriate to talk about God in personal terms. In many of the Hebrew myths God is spoken of as if God is a big person: God walks in the garden in the heat of the day, makes a mark on the face of Cain, and has a home in heaven which is threatened by the humans building their tower at Babel. This speech about God as in some sense personal continues throughout the scriptures. On the other hand, the wind of God moves over the water and gives life to all creatures, so God is also depicted as a form of energy. And sometimes God is referred to as a rock, or a fortress, and appears as fire or cloud, all of which are very impersonal.

This squares with the variety of experiences of the Transcendent which we considered in chapter 5. There are Christian mystics like Julian of Norwich, for whom God is very personal, but others, like Meister Eckhart, for whom God is less so. Similarly, among people describing their religious experiences to researchers there is difference and variety. Among those who experience the Transcendent in nature there are those who are awed by a desert, the sea, or the vastness of a clear sky, and this is completely impersonal. But other people are comforted, rested or energised by being among trees or on open moorland, as they might hope to be if they were with a caring parent or friend.

Rudolph Otto's preferred term for what people experience at these times was 'the Numinous', which is a neutral term, and yet for Martin Buber, the essential encounter with the Divine was in I-Thou relationships between people. For him, it was in the intensely personal. This variety in both the scriptures and the breadth of human experience suggests that speaking of God as a person or as a thing are both at times appropriate, but also both inadequate. No terms for God adequately point to or symbolise what we are speaking of. As an ancient Hindu teaching puts it: God is both that and not that.

In what follows I will try to simply refer to 'God' and to avoid using pronouns. To use a variety of terms such as the Transcendent, the One, or the Holy, becomes cumbersome. To speak of God as he, she or it is inadequate, and it is confusing if we interchange the pronouns. So I will use the traditional Hebrew and Christian ways of speaking about God as personal, but with a rider that thinking of God as a force, energy, or power, is at times much more appropriate. God is not a person or a thing. God is God, and what God is in Godself we do not know.

Chapter 13

Creation now:
Cosmic art

In the Hebrew scriptures God creates the world but the Hebrew writers conceived of the world very differently from us. We know the earth is not set upon pillars with water around and under it, and covered by a dome. The earth is a small planet circling the sun in a galaxy which is one among billions in an expanding universe.

Another cosmology

However, even though the cosmos is expanding and continually changing, in another sense it is remarkably balanced. As we noted in chapter 2, there are several essential constants which if they were different by a tiny fraction of a percentage would mean that after the Big Bang the whole cosmos would have collapsed in on itself or rapidly expanded into cold infinity. For the cosmos to exist at all, let alone have characteristics which have enabled life to develop on the earth and perhaps also on other planets, calls for some remarkably fine tuning.[1] Some cosmologists believe that the world we have is the outcome of random chance: in other words, that left long enough, and there is an infinite amount of time available, a universe such as ours will appear. Other cosmologists reckon that is literally incredible. They say it cannot have just happened but has a cause of some sort: there must be a creator.[2]

This is known as the cosmological argument for the existence of God and it has been around for a long time. Ultimately it cannot be proved that the universe is created. Perhaps, in the same way that a sequence of sounds can be recognised as music, paint on a canvas as art, or ink on paper as literature, it is a way of seeing the world. And to me, it makes sense that there is more to the cosmos than random, accidental matter, and that what is behind it, like a composer, an artist or a writer, is what we mean by 'God'.[3]

We can develop further these images of art, music and literature.

Think of a piece of graffiti art, like a Banksy, painted on a concrete wall. The texture of the wall is visible through the painting, and the wall extends beyond the picture. Usually it is the picture we notice rather than the concrete, in the same way that most of the time we notice and pay attention to the world. But, without the wall there would be no picture.

Before a concert begins there is a silence, which extends after it, and lies behind the music. Mozart reckoned that the silences within music were as important as the sounds themselves. In fact, without silence the music could become another noise. Perhaps God is like the silence in which the symphony of the cosmos plays.[4]

Here, what you are reading is ink on paper or words on a screen, and hopefully it is conjuring up some meaning for you. Much has gone into this that you do not see, in the study, research, thinking, discussion, and writing. My hope is that what I write will encourage your own thinking and influence your feelings and actions. A book is so much more than paper and ink, or light on a screen, and the cosmos is more than matter.

The world is much more than what we see, feel, measure and shape. As Creator, God might be thought of as the artist, the composer, or the author of the cosmos. The scriptures also suggest God is at work within time and space. The cosmos is not a finished work, neither is it a great machine but a myriad of interconnections and an interplay of structure and chance. God might also be thought of as within that, or behind that, like the beauty of a painting or the meaning of text, not to be seen in a chemical analysis of the material, but recognised in the whole.

A matter of size

Considering the vastness of the cosmos and the billions of years of its existence, how can God be interested in us on this small planet at this period in time? The writers of the Hebrew scriptures spoke of God not only being interested in us but even wanting to have some kind of relationship with us.

As we have seen, it is not clear whether Genesis 1 suggests God shapes the chaos that is there before God creates, or whether God calls the world into existence from nothing. But, whichever is meant, it is very clear that God is not considered part of the world that is created. God is beyond it, within it, and expresses Godself in creating and in relating to it. Put into our terms: God is not caught up in the space-time continuum. And if that is the case, distance is of no consequence, and neither is time.[5]

That is not totally alien to our experience. A woman may own ten thousand acres of land but her small engagement ring might be of more significance to her than all the fields. An experiment can be conducted at the CERN laboratory and the crucial event the scientists are focussed on will take place in a nanosecond, but the experiment was years in the planning, the laboratory took decades to design and build, and the thinking behind the project goes back centuries. Similarly, size and duration will not necessarily be significant for God if God transcends both space and time.

In the mythological creation poem in Genesis 1 God calls things into existence and 'sees they are good'. There is an idea here of God appreciating the world that God is creating. There is a similar sense in the older story in Genesis 2 where God 'walks in the garden in the cool of the evening'. It is as if God is out for a stroll and happens to come across the man and woman. Both images are rather quaint, but if astrophysicists can get excited about galaxies, nebulae, and black holes, and many of us enjoy looking at the pictures being returned from space probes, why should the Creator not enjoy the whole cosmos, rather than just the bit of it that we are on? And why should there not be living beings on other planets which can have a sense of the Creator and with whom the Creator can have a two-way relationship?

Pain and injustice

But, if God is interested in and cares about this small planet, why on earth is there pain and injustice? An old theology said these were the result of the Fall but that does not work. Firstly, as I suggested in chapter 8, the idea of a historical Fall treats myths as if they are descriptions of events. It also does not answer the problem, as has been pointed out many times: God must have created the Devil who caused the problem.[6]

We know that humans developed from earlier primates and that long before *Homo sapiens* developed there were animals feeling pain. The idea of a state in which all animals only eat things that cannot feel is lovely but it is impossible: a lion or tiger that ate only plants would be a different animal. It would have a different physical structure, metabolism, and genetic code. And predators are a necessary part of an ecosystem. There was no paradise before the first humans ate a fruit in a garden and it seems that pain is built into the living matrix of life.

Pain is sometimes helpful. Painful illnesses are terrible, but so too are illnesses where feeling is lost. In biblical times 'leprosy' was a greatly feared illness. This was quite possibly Hansen's disease, a bacterial infection which attacks the nerves and causes loss of feeling, and deformities result from people injuring themselves through lack of sensitivity. Pain is also sometimes a helpful warning of a developing disease which can be remedied if it is attended to.

Also, much of the pain in the human world arises from human action or inaction. As I write, people are responding to an earthquake in Turkey and Syria which has killed thousands and injured many more. Much of that suffering was the result not of the earthquake, which was simply the shifting of the earth's tectonic plates, but of bad construction and siting of buildings. Wars are a consequence of human decisions, plain and simple.

Nevertheless, having said that, we need to acknowledge that pain is experienced by many living creatures and it is not always helpful. It is not always caused by other people nor by accidents. And it is not distributed fairly. One person might live for eighty years in relative comfort while another lives for a few days in great pain.[7]

Suffering pain is a fact of life and many great minds have wrestled with how it can be reconciled with belief in a Creator God. We will return to the subject, holding it for now as an unanswered question, as it was in most of the Hebrew scriptures. The writer of Job addressed it, and gave a non-answer but a powerful response. The author of Ecclesiastes saw it as another indicator of the futility of human life. Writers of the Psalms sometimes threw their anger at God, while others trusted there must be an answer somewhere: not so much an intellectual answer or a solution but a resolution.

This brings us back to the question of hope. It is because we are not satisfied with the injustice and suffering of the present time, and because we anticipate further suffering by other creatures in the future, that we ask what hope there might be. It is because we enjoy beauty and pleasure that we abhor ugliness and pain. It is because we have an innate or even articulated belief that the world is good that we resist brutality, violence, and the needless destruction of life. And as we do all this we look for hope.

Living art

The Hebrew scriptures suggest that humanity is created to reflect the character of the creative, caring God, and to have a conscious relationship with God. They also suggest that God wants a form of justice in human society which involves caring for the needy and sharing power with the powerless. God wants humanity to show this aspect of God's character to the other forms of life on the earth and failure to do so elicits God's condemnation and remedial action.

If the universe is God's creation then the beauty and mystery of the world are not simply coincidental or accidental but integral to its existence. This would be why many people find encounters with 'nature' helpful, healing, pleasurable or restorative, in the same way as others might find a visit to an art gallery, a festival or a concert. The natural world can be thought of as a work of art. If the cosmos is created, we might expect to encounter the Creator through nature like we encounter an artist in their work.

Not all encounters with nature are healing or restorative. Some are terrifying. Others are deadly. Nature may be said to be 'good', but it is itself and we are just a part of it. Frightening encounters with nature remind us of our relative frailty in contrast to our often grandiose ideas of human significance, and sometimes they bring us face to face with our mortality. This is also true of other experiences of transcendence. They too can sometimes remind us of the limitations of human understanding and knowledge, of our mortality, and of the deep mysteries of living and dying.

Hope and humanity

If humanity is created by God to reflect God's character, as Genesis suggests, then the awe, joy and creativity that we experience as part of the world are essential aspects of our being. It also means that our frustration, passion and anger about the destruction of life on the earth might be an echo of the frustration, passion and anger of God.[8]

As pictured in the Hebrew scriptures, humanity was to have a conscious relationship with God which involves choice. It is part of our experience to be able to make decisions, and we observe the oppression, captivity or enslavement of people as abhorrent because we have a deep sense that people should be free.

At the same time, we know too that all our freedom is limited. As individuals our physical and mental capacities restrict what we can do. Our obligations and our relationship with other people place further restrictions on us. And there are the social dynamics we are caught up in as well as our personal and social histories which influence us. Despite this we still have a sense that we are all entitled to some freedom of choice, and that to take this away is to dehumanise us.

That means we are in a paradoxical situation. We expect ourselves and others to have some freedom of choice, while we are also anxious that we and others will choose to do what is good for ourselves, society and the earth. We fear both constraint and disorder. We desperately want what is good but we also believe people should be free not to choose it, and are sometimes afraid that they will not do good.

We thought in chapter 2 about how with the physical phenomenon of chaos something which is seemingly random can have, at a higher level, a degree of order. We also know that out of the interplay of order with random mutation there has developed not only life, but intelligence and self-awareness.

We can conceive of God as both beyond and within space, time and matter, and also continually creating the cosmos and active in each moment of time. As Creator, God would not be one factor in the complex interplay of life and humanity, but would transcend it. God would not be a player in the orchestra but the composer. God would not be an actor in the play but the playwright or director. And if this is so, there is hope for life on the earth, and for humanity.[9]

The image this suggests is not of God outside the world, occasionally interfering. Nor of God being in the world as one of the many forces pushing and pulling within it. But of the world being within God and God within the world: God both transcendent and immanent, not just being but also doing. At work. Continually creating. Continually healing. Beyond and within space and time, within the matrices of life and in the creativity, imagination, and compassion of humans.

For the future

What such a relationship between God and the world means for the future of human society we could not expect to be able to foresee, but the scriptures suggest some patterns. In the Torah, the Psalms and the Prophets God does not simply mourn the enslavement, dehumanisation, and destruction of people, but works to heal and to liberate. This involves the condemnation of injustices, a reordering of societies, and new orders being created; all of which are not without pain.

We have already noted how we and other individuals are not as free to act as we would sometimes wish. Also, although it runs counter to the post-Enlightenment myth of the free individual, it is part of our experience that we individuals are part of larger groups: families, communities, societies, and so on. In the scriptures it is frequently not individuals who are liberated or condemned but societies.

That suggests that our hope probably lies not along an easy or comfortable path but will involve the painful restructuring of the present social systems which are leading to the destruction of life and humanity. And that those who care for the wellbeing of the earth's life, and with it the wellbeing of humanity, will be involved in a struggle. However, as they are acting in accord with the values, purposes and ways of God it is not hopeless. And the scriptures also suggest something of the shape of that hope.

Chapter 14

A dynamic Trinity:
Creative, expressive, active

The fourth gospel, the Gospel According to John, famously begins with a poem which echoes the opening verses of Genesis. However, John's focus is on God's expression of Godself. In Genesis God speaks and a world comes into existence. In John, the Word of God becomes a person: Jesus.[1]

Before John's Gospel was written there were in the Christian writings such phrases as Paul's 'The grace of our Lord Jesus Christ, the love of God and the fellowship of the Holy Spirit' (2 Corinthians 13.13); and also possibly predating John, the command at the end of Matthew to baptise in the name of the Father, the Son and the Holy Spirit.[2] In the synoptic gospels and some of the early letters Jesus is referred to as 'son of God', a phrase originally applied to a king of Israel; and 'the Lord', which is a term of respect for a powerful person or for God. John's language reinforced this sense of connection between God beyond the world, God within it, and the man Jesus, and this developed into what became known as the doctrine of the Trinity.

Three and one

Unfortunately, this idea is sometimes dangled before church congregations as a great intellectual puzzle which they cannot solve. Some churches have a special day dedicated to thinking about the Trinity, and there are clergy who would rather not preach that day because they find it so difficult. But surely the idea comes from people experiencing God in different ways: as the origin of everything that is, as the energy within what exists, and in the insights people receive into how God is and what matters to God. Turn that around and we could say that God is beyond everything, within everything, and also expresses Godself: these are different experiences of different aspects of God, but all one God.

It was unfortunate for Western Christian theology that the term *persona* was used for these three aspects of God. A *persona* was a mask in

Greek theatre but the word came in Western thinking to mean an individual: in the English language, a person. So it was that later Christians were baffled by how one God could be three persons, and Jews, and later Muslims, came to think of Christians as splitting the One and indivisible.

A basic problem is that all talk about God tends to make us think of God as a thing among things, or an object among other objects, or a person among other persons. The idea that the world is created by God, and that every thing, every object, and every person exists because of God, should counter that tendency, but it does not necessarily do so. A lot of Christian religious talk and prayer goes on as if God is one being among many.

Metaphors and mystics

All talk about God is going to be metaphorical. The words create mental images and no image is completely satisfactory. Down the centuries many mystics have tried to remind people of this, and in so doing often got into trouble with Church authorities. Meister Eckhart, for example, is now widely recognised as a great teacher but was charged with heresy in his time. Mystics have also sometimes not been popular with church congregations, or at least with people who want a simple faith and straight answers to straight questions.

But if the nature of the universe is not simple, how can we expect the nature of God to be simple? What we have are verbal images, metaphors, stories, poems, and aphorisms all pointing towards God, with the proviso that none of them is totally adequate. So it is that some mystics have followed a path known as apophatic theology, or a *via negativa*, which involves speaking instead about what God is not, and leading ultimately to a cloud of unknowing.

Sam Keen said, 'I am not uncomfortable in saying that my trust in the ultimate context of my life is invested in God, provided the word "God" is not used more than once a year and is then handled like the Ark of the Covenant'[3]

In the 1950s Paul Tillich developed a systematic theology using concepts from existentialist philosophy and wrote about 'the Ground of

Being'. For a while that became a popular alternative to 'God' in some Christian circles and even made its way into some hymnbooks.[4] It provided a useful counterweight to the idea of God as a Celestial Schoolmaster, laying down his rules and marking homework. Or the Helpful Friend who finds you a parking space at the supermarket. Or as the benign Old Man up there looking down on us. But Tillich's phrase has not made it into mainstream Christian liturgy.

He also spoke about 'the God beyond the God of theism'.[5] This is possibly an oxymoron as any belief in God is going to still be theism, however many stages of transcendence God is thought to be beyond. But it points in the direction of God not being a thing, an entity, a substance, or an object. It is because of God that things, entities, substances and objects exist.

Metaphors of unity

Numerous teachers and preachers down the centuries have spoken about the Trinity as if it was like three players in one team, three ingredients in one cake, or three leaves on one shamrock stem.[6] But what the Hebrew and Christian scriptures point to is God creating everything that is, the Spirit moving like the wind over the sea and giving life to matter, and God speaking through prophets, seers, wise people, and in the life, words, death and resurrection of Jesus. They are not three of the same kind of thing, but three aspects of the One ultimate reality.

It is more like talking about 'music', which can refer to a score, to sounds, or to the experience of involvement and engagement with the sounds being made. Or like 'poetry', which is words on paper, and the sound as someone reads the poem, and the images and emotions the words conjure up. Or like a 'party', which is a group of people with food and drink, an atmosphere, and a celebration.

If God is beyond everything, and within everything, and also expresses Godself within the Creation, then having an idea of God being above us, in the heavens, or below us, as the ground of our being, has severe limitations. God being Trinity suggests not us being under, or beside, or even above God, but us being within God: like being in a house, or better still in a forest, or being like a fish in an ocean, or a dancer in a festival, or a musician in a symphony.[7]

Belief and faith

It is probably unfortunate that some churches have a habit of reciting one of their creeds at every service. 'I believe in God', the people say. Or, 'We believe in One God, the Father Almighty,' and so on. These were not written to be used in liturgy. The first, the so-called Apostles' Creed, began its life as the curriculum for a baptism preparation course. The second was a position statement from a Church conference. But the principal word that gives rise to misunderstanding, is the word 'believe'.

The creeds begin, 'believe in …' not 'believe that …'. The person reciting the creed is not saying that they believe that there is a god, as if there exists one of a certain kind of thing called gods. They are not even saying that they believe there is God.

The word 'believe' crops up frequently in the Christian scriptures, which were all originally written in Greek. When they were first translated into English the word 'believe' was used to translate the Greek *pisteo* and has continued to be used ever since. But *pisteo* does not mean to believe something to be true. It means to trust something or someone.

In English it is possible to say, 'I have faith' but that is never said in Greek. Faith, *pistis*, is not something you have but something you do. So when in some translations of the gospels Jesus says to someone that they should 'have faith' it would be better translated as 'trust me', or 'trust God'. Or simply, 'Trust!'[8]

It is notable that while some traditional Church creeds go on at length about who Jesus is with regard to God 'the Father', Jesus never once in the gospels says to someone asking for his help, 'Do you believe that I am the Son of God?' or 'The Messiah?' or 'the Word Incarnate?', or whatever. He commends faith and does not look for belief in that sense.[9]

God's concerns

But why would one trust God? The basis of Hebrew faith was how God had acted in the past, which shows God's concerns in the present. Jews look back to God's liberating the people from their slavery in Egypt and making a covenant with them at Mount Sinai. So, in Jesus' time, if he was seen as working on behalf of God he could be expected to bring liberation, in one way or another. The healings he carried out, and his defence of 'sinners' against the condemnation of the self-righteous, were acts of liberation.

Many Jews then as now, and certainly Jesus and his followers, also paid heed to the proclamations and teaching of the Prophets. They believed God was concerned for the poor and downtrodden. God would work to bring justice, and to create a peace in which people could thrive. Though God was God, the Creator of 'the heavens and the earth', God was not emotionally distant but cared about people. And not just God's own people, the Jews, but others too. In the Psalms God is also described as providing food for the wild animals and birds.[10]

The book of Jonah is a tale about a man who is told to go and prophesy in Nineveh so the people can change their lives and avoid the disaster that is heading their way. Jonah is reluctant to do so and gets on a ship in the opposite direction. But there is a storm, Jonah is thrown overboard and he is swallowed by a great fish, or in children's books, a whale, which is much more fun. God rescues him, so he eventually goes to Nineveh and half-heartedly preaches that the people should repent. They do, and they wear sackcloth and ashes accordingly, even dressing their animals in these rags of repentance. Disaster is averted, and Jonah sulks.

The real prophet, of course, was not a man called Jonah but the person who wrote the story. The writer saw God as being concerned for the good of people, even the people of the dreadful city of Nineveh, and wanting their welfare not their punishment.

Love and judgement

There is an idea in some Christian circles that God in the Old Testament is a giver of rules and of punishments for those who do not keep them, whereas in the New Testament God is loving, gentle and nice. As a result, the Old Testament is rarely read in their churches from one year to the next, except for the bits at Christmas which they think talk about Jesus coming. In the second century there was a Christian teacher called Marcion who taught just that and produced his own edition of the Bible with parts of Luke and Paul's letters, and none of the Hebrew scriptures. Marcion is long dead but the attitude lives on. But it is mistaken. To quote from just a few Psalms:

I will sing of your steadfast love, O Lord, for ever;
  with my mouth I will proclaim your faithfulness to all generations.
I declare that your steadfast love is established for ever;
  your faithfulness is as firm as the heavens. (Psalm 89.1–2)
Praise the Lord, all you nations!
  Extol him, all you peoples!
For great is his steadfast love towards us,
  and the faithfulness of the Lord endures for ever. (Psalm 117.1–2)

The Lord is gracious and merciful,
  slow to anger and abounding in steadfast love.
The Lord is good to all,
  and his compassion is over all that he has made. (Psalm 145.8–9)

It is certainly the case that in the Hebrew scriptures there is talk about God judging the people. Prophets warn of forthcoming catastrophes as a consequence of disobedience or a lack of loyalty to God. God wants justice, a concern for the suffering, poor and oppressed, and wants action to help them, but that is often lacking in society. God wants righteousness, people living in a right relationship with God and with each other, but often they are not. Prophets speak, demanding change, but often their calls are ignored and so eventually God acts to bring about change, to remove the obstacles and sometimes to drastically restructure the society. That is what some Jews during the Exile came to see God as having done in letting their land be invaded by the Babylonians.

Flickering hope

Some of the writers of the Hebrew scriptures were very clear that this did not explain all suffering and pain. There were certainly some who glibly said that bad things happened to bad people and good things to good people, and there were some at the time of Jesus who thought that too. However, there were many writers who realised that was not the case.

The Hebrews had a very strong sense of people being embedded in families and communities. Because of this they perhaps had less indignation than we might have about innocent individuals who were collateral damage in a disaster which had been brought on by a ruling elite. The great grief was for the society as a whole, of which they were a part.

Nevertheless, there were also clearly many times when good individuals suffered injustices which were not rectified, or illnesses, injuries and griefs which they did not seem to merit, and this caused anger or indignation. Stuff happened then as it happens now, and people were not naive. Nevertheless, many of them hung on in faith and hope that things somehow would be put right, as people often do now. It is a flickering hope which can perhaps be strengthened when we think about what happened to Jesus. While there may not be a solution, there may be stronger reason to hope.

Chapter 15

God and us:
Love and suffering

Thinking about suffering and God would not be a problem if we did not have an idea that God loves humanity and the rest of the Creation. In many mythologies and religions there are gods who do not love but are simply concerned with their own affairs. Humans are perhaps their playthings, or simply suffer collateral damage in the struggles between one god and another. But the Hebrew and Christian scriptures suggest that God cares about the world, so suffering is a problem.

Immeasurable pain

To put it blandly, there is a lot of suffering in the world. Pain ranges from the pain of illnesses like appendicitis which can be rectified to chronic nerve disorders which keep people in constant pain for years. Suffering ranges from the deprivation of a child through poverty in Britain to thousands of people held in camps for re-education in China; from an assault on a woman in an American subway to the Russian bombing of a city in Ukraine; from a single rabbit dying from myxomatosis in England to the destruction of a whole ecosystem in South America. It cannot be measured.

In thinking about how much suffering there is in the world we should perhaps also remember that there is also a great deal of pleasure, fun, laughter, and joy. That too cannot be measured, so there is no question of working out whether the pleasure and joy balances out the pain and suffering. However, most people probably reckon that pleasure outweighs pain over all, and though some people decide that the pain is overwhelming and they would be better off without a life at all, most want to continue to live.

We humans are able to anticipate what might happen, which is both an asset and a problem. We are not the only creatures that can do this but we are very good at it. It enables us to plan, to avoid danger and unnecessary suffering, and to create good and beneficial situations for ourselves and others. But it also means that we can anticipate possible pain, which can add to our suffering. The problem of a slight pain is amplified by the thought that it might get worse and it could be something serious. During a pandemic we wonder whether we will be next. Or, watching news reports of a war we can not only feel for the people involved but also wonder how it will develop and how it might affect us.

God and the suffering world

We have thought about how some of the suffering in the world is stuff that just happens by natural causes, how some is a downside of something that seemed like a good idea at the time, and how some of it is deliberately caused by people. How does this relate to God who is allegedly the creator of the cosmos and is said to love it? I am not going to try to resolve this profound question in a few paragraphs but some points from the ponderings of thinkers over the centuries are worth noting. They do not solve the intellectual problem but might make a difference to how we view it.

One is that suffering gives an opportunity for other people to care. Often we notice a lack of care, but there is also in the world a great deal of care and compassion, much of which is taken for granted. If compassion and love are valuable it is hard to see how they could flourish in a world without problems.

A second point is whether the world could have been different. We know now the constants which mean that this cosmos has neither collapsed in on itself nor rapidly expanded into a desert of atoms but has enabled life to develop on this small planet and possibly others. Could there have been a cosmos which did that but which did not have the existence of pain and suffering and the possibilities of cruelty among intelligent beings? We do not know. Perhaps not.

A third point is that being time-bound creatures we can think of the world as 'going somewhere'. Or as parts of it going somewhere. An old image is to think of human life as a pilgrimage, and whether it is to the Celestial City, as with Bunyan's Christian, or towards individuation, as suggested by Jungian psychology, the trials of life give opportunity for growth and development. J.S. Bach's music is extraordinarily balanced and mathematical and yet there are many occasions of discord. The discordance enriches the music because it is in transit, and is eventually resolved. Maybe life is like music which breaks for a while into discord but eventually resolves.

A fourth way of thinking about the suffering in the world is to blame it on the Devil. The world has sometimes been seen as a battleground between two evenly balanced forces of good and evil, or the Devil and his cohorts have been seen as rebels against the rightful rule of God. Such views have been influential down the centuries of Christian thinking, probably more in popular religion than in academic theology, and they have had some dreadful consequences. They have led to witch-hunts, the demonising of minorities, and fears which have enabled power to be abused.

But in the drama of the Christian scriptures the Devil, or Satan, is a minor player. Jesus is tested by the Devil, and talks about a crippled woman being bound by Satan; he sees Simon Peter as a mouthpiece for Satan when he suggests that he can avoid suffering, and Jesus' opponents reckon that he is working for Satan.[1] But that was part of the world view of the time.

In Paul's letters the problem is not Satan, but sin.[2] In the apocalyptic fantasy the book of Revelation, the Devil features as one of the enemies to be overcome by God.[3] But, as we have noted, in the stories and poems of creation there is no mention of a Devil.[4]

Responsibility

Talk about the Devil can be a smokescreen for human irresponsibility. In the Torah people are told how they are to live and that as part of the covenant they are responsible for keeping God's commands. Prophets remind people time and again that God will judge society when it fails to live with justice and righteousness. There is no talk of a Devil causing oppression, violence or dishonesty. People are responsible for what they do.

Judgement is a two-edged word. For the poor and oppressed, judgement is liberation. For the wealthy and oppressive, it is destruction.

The judges in the law courts, which in ancient Palestine were the city gates, were to protect the poor from the ravages and depredations of the powerful. That was the idea, and it was what a good judge did. According to the Prophets, it was what God, the ultimate judge, would do if they failed.

We can identify with that idea of justice, albeit in our much more complex society. We see powerful and enormously wealthy organisations holding even nation states to ransom, to allow them to exploit their 'resources' or to make them pay their 'debts'. The people of the Niger Delta have great difficulty getting Shell to pay anything towards repairing the environmental destruction they have caused by oil spills and drilling. A local council in England sometimes cannot resist a planning application by a major supermarket chain because the supermarket has more money and can keep reapplying until, in the end, the legal costs make the council withdraw. People in England are theoretically protected from defamation by libel laws, but only the very wealthy can afford the lawyers' fees to make a claim. And so we look for justice, for deliverance, and protection.

Sin and judgement

We acknowledged in chapter 3 how even the powerful are constrained in what they are able to do by the systems that they are caught up in, or by their own weaknesses and emotional wounds. We could see this as being another way of describing what Paul meant when he talked about sin as a malign power constraining people. We often find ourselves in a tension between our own freedom of choice and the internal constraints upon us. We know that our past experiences, the systems we are part of, our fears for ourselves and other people, and our weaknesses, all influence how we respond to the situations we find ourselves in, but we also know we often have a choice.

Down the centuries different theologians have emphasised one side or another of this tension. Following the classic struggle in the fifth century between Augustine of Hippo and Pelagius, Augustine's views became mainstream and greatly influenced the Reformers, especially Martin Luther and John Calvin.[5] Pelagianism was branded a heresy but

Pelagius' theology was much more subtle than his critics reported and his fundamental argument, that it is unjust of God to condemn people for doing something they cannot help, is hard to refute.

The idea of God as judge has been abused down the years, and the medieval pictures of a terrible judge condemning unbelievers and sinners to the perpetual torture of demons are a masterclass in propaganda for the advantage of the clerics who claimed the power to forgive sins. But if we follow Jesus' teaching we can see God as a judge who does not operate mechanically, like an inspector ticking boxes, but like a parent who knows the strengths and weaknesses of their children, or like a shepherd who knows the idiosyncrasies of their sheep.[6] Any decent teacher adjusts demands to the capabilities of a child. Sports trainers consider carefully the strengths, weaknesses and possibilities of their trainees.

Suffering God

When Jesus came into Galilee preaching that the reign of God was at hand many people thought that the time of God's judgement was about to come. Their suffering would be relieved, their problems sorted, and injustices rectified. They would be set free from their wage slavery. The mighty would be put down and the poor raised up.[7] That did not all happen, but Jesus' followers still believed him to be God's anointed king: a messiah. We have already thought about what did happen.[8] The question is how we can understand in our terms what happened after Jesus' arrest.

The gospel writers have their different emphases and details but the basic account is the same. We do not know anything about the past lives of most of the main characters and the gospel writers had little interest in exploring the characters' underlying or unconscious motives. That was not a concern in their culture. But in the attitude to Jesus of those with political power we see the fear of people who saw Jesus as a threat. We see the ideological blinkers of people who cannot conceive that this preacher from Galilee was a messiah. We see people lying for their own advantage. And when he is handed over to Pilate the imperial system crushes him. Whatever Pilate felt or thought personally about Jesus, the Empire mattered more and possible rebels needed to be destroyed.[9]

Jesus was condemned, flogged, and crucified. It was a grave injustice, painful and humiliating. And as he died he is said to have called out, 'My God, why have you forsaken me?' He felt abandoned by God. Cursed, as the Torah put it.[10]

But if Jesus was, as Paul puts it, 'the image of the invisible God'; if, as the Letter to the Hebrews puts it, 'God has spoken to us by a Son'; or if, as John's Gospel puts it, Jesus is 'the Word made flesh', we see here something more of what God is like. God suffers.[11]

To take those sayings seriously means seeing God not only in Jesus' healings of people, but in his suffering and dying. Hearing God not only in Jesus' parables and words of forgiveness, but in his cry of abandonment.

Beyond compassion

For centuries Christian theology was dominated by a Greek idea that God must be beyond suffering. So it was that the death of Jesus was seen as something carried out according to God's will, but his suffering was the suffering of the man Jesus. However, God in the Hebrew scriptures is far from being the apathetic God of Greek philosophy and Christian scholasticism. God is one who cares about people, who is grieved by their turning away, and who is moved in compassion for the slaves in Egypt. Compassion means to 'suffer with'.

In the twentieth century there was a change in some Christian thinking. We might call it a realisation: a realisation that Jesus shows that God suffers. And this is not simply compassion, or a deep sympathy, but a suffering experienced by God in Jesus.

First World War chaplain Geoffrey Studdert Kennedy wrote:

How can it be that God can reign in glory,
Calmly content with what His Love has done,
Reading unmoved the piteous shameful story,
All the vile deeds men do beneath the sun?
Are there no tears in the heart of the Eternal?
Is there no pain to pierce the soul of God?
Then must He be a fiend of Hell infernal,
Beating the earth to pieces by His rod.[12]

Dietrich Bonhoeffer, in prison in 1944, wrote in a letter to a friend:

> Only a suffering God can help us now.[13]

In 1973 Jürgen Moltmann wrote:

> 'God is unconditional love, because he takes on himself grief at the contradiction in [humanity] and does not angrily suppress this contradiction. God allows himself to be forced out. God suffers, God allows himself to be crucified and is crucified, and in this consummates his unconditional love that is so full of hope.'[14]

To these writers, God suffers from human injustice. God suffers with the Creation.

God in darkness

Our questioning now about hope, our concern for our society, perhaps for our children and grandchildren, and our awareness of what is going on that threatens not just human society but much life on the planet, might lead us into mental and emotional darkness. If it does, it is a darkness we share with others, and with God.

For many people it is not just concern and anxiety that draw them into the darkness but real pain, hunger, the failure of rains, the destruction of homes and livelihoods in storms or warfare, holding dying children, or the endless struggle with poverty. God is suffering in that darkness.

We can think of the world as being continually created by God who is beyond matter, space and time, and also within the whole cosmos from its origins to its end. We can think of God caring about it in all its vastness, and also concerned for life on this small blue planet. We can think of God suffering with it and suffering within it.

It is not an explanation: it is a way of thinking, a way of seeing, perhaps an awareness, or a sense we might have about the depth, wonder, mystery, and pain of our lives and of our world. There are always more questions, and there is certainly more to be said. But we can also pause with that idea: that God suffers with us and with the rest of creation. Or with that image: of Jesus on the cross showing something of the pain of God.

Chapter 16

New creation:
Life out of death

Earlier, in chapters 10 and 11, we thought about the synoptic gospels being legendary in the sense that they contain stories and sayings which altered over time. Unlike many legends which were told over many generations before being written down there was just one generation between the events and the writing.[1] But in that time the stories were told often, and not just for entertainment. They were the basis of preaching and of teaching in the emergent Christian movement.

The gospels are also mythical, in the sense that they have shaped people's attitudes, ideas and feelings, but unlike the myths of Baldur and Odin, and like Bannockburn, the Boston Tea Party, and the Fall of the Bastille, they have history behind them, even though the exact details can no longer be ascertained.

The overall gospel story does not stop with the death of Jesus. In their different ways the four gospels and the letters in the New Testament tell of Jesus 'being raised from the dead'. There are good reasons for considering that this too is part of the historic bedrock: the fundamental change in the disciples from cowering peasants to courageous preachers, his appearances to some of his disciples, and the empty tomb.

All historic events are unique. There have been plenty of rebellions, demonstrations and battles but, it is said, there has only been one resurrection. According to the gospels Jesus on three occasions recalled someone back to life: a widow's son in Nain, Jairus' daughter, and Lazarus.[2] But these were resuscitations. These people would die again one day. What was claimed about Jesus was something quite different.

The resurrection of Jesus

In the sequel to Luke's Gospel, the Acts of the Apostles, the change in the disciples was attributed to the work of the Holy Spirit, the energy of God. Jesus who had been killed was now alive with the life of God and at work by the Spirit of God. His mission was continuing now through his disciples who were energised by the Spirit, and they were like 'the body of Christ', to use one of Paul's phrases.[3] This energy was the same energy that in the Hebrew scriptures is said to move over the waters of chaos, to give life continually to the creatures on earth, to have inspired prophets and anointed kings, and empowered Jesus himself.

The second basis for the claim that Jesus had 'risen' were the appearances of Jesus to his disciples. They are described in different ways in the gospels, Acts and Paul's letters. Paul speaks about a light from heaven, while Luke talks about a fellow traveller joining two disciples on the road, with no light and no special voice. John has Jesus joining the disciples in a locked room, and later by the lakeshore. Matthew has him appearing to the disciples on a mountaintop. They are all highly symbolic tales, told and retold many times. But experiences of the Transcendent are notoriously difficult to describe, and all strange tales get changed over time. We have no way of examining the disciples' experiences although clearly something happened which convinced them Jesus was risen and gave them the courage to speak out about it.

There was seen to be a strong link between the resurrection appearances and the Spirit of God. John has Jesus promise his disciples another 'helper' after his departure, and then when he appears to them he breathes on them and says 'Receive the Holy Spirit'. Matthew has Jesus declare that he himself will be with them 'to the close of the ages'. Luke has Jesus go into heaven, and then has the Spirit come from heaven dramatically like wind and fire. Paul has Jesus and the Spirit so linked that he can talk, on occasion, about the Spirit of Jesus.[4] The suggestion clearly is that the appearances came to an end but the Spirit remained.

Among the many religious experiences we thought about in chapter 5, the appearances of the risen Jesus and of the empowering Spirit must stand out as among some of the most historically influential. Whatever it was that happened to the disciples, it changed them and they and their successors began to change society. However, while that event was unique, the creative Spirit of God is not tied to one time, place, or institution.

An empty tomb?

The third basis for belief in the resurrection of Jesus was the empty tomb, and it is this that is particularly challenging. Put bluntly, people who are dead and buried stay in their graves. However, we have already thought in chapter 11 about the problems with dismissing the story of the empty tomb. It remains a historical mystery.

Down the years many people have argued that the tomb was empty. Many, if not most, have been driven by the belief that it must have happened because it says so in the Bible. But not everyone has argued on that basis. Wolfhart Pannenberg suggested in the 1960s that it cannot be dismissed on the basis of scientific laws because these laws describe what happens and do not determine it, and the Resurrection was a unique event.[5]

The relevant science, of course, is not just the simple statement that dead people stay dead. There is the whole question of matter and space. What happened to the material of Jesus' body? But the evidence, Pannenberg says, points to the tomb being empty, however hard it is to understand what might have happened.

Whether or not the tomb was empty, and it is notable that Paul never mentioned it, it is still reasonable to think about the Resurrection as an event. The change in the disciples, linked with their experience of the risen Jesus and the empowering of the Spirit, constituted a happening which arguably was as historical as, and of greater significance than, the Battle of Bannockburn or the French or American Revolutions. It gave rise to the whole Christian movement which has profoundly affected world history.

The reign of God and the church

But what happened to the reign of God that Jesus spoke about? He had allegedly preached in Nazareth that he was anointed by God to bring good news to the poor and let the oppressed go free.[6] But poverty and oppression have continued down the history of the world. The church's track record in dealing with poverty and oppression has been very mixed. Any balanced history book will include both St Francis and the

Borgias, Martin Luther King and Hendrik Verwoerd, Mother Teresa and the Magdalene Laundries.

It has sometimes been claimed that the church is the fulfilment of the reign of God but, given the church's record, that must be nonsense, and it was clearly so from the beginning. Paul had harsh words to say to the church in Corinth about their arrogance and their marginalisation of poor people. When Paul spoke about the reign, or kingdom, of God it was to say that it was 'righteousness and peace and joy in the Holy Spirit'.[7] Clearly, for him, the kingdom was something that should be realised in a congregation but could not be taken for granted.

The energy of God

When Jesus went around Galilee preaching that the reign of God was at hand a lot of people thought that the time had come for God to sort out the mess: to relieve the poverty, remove the oppressive Romans, give the wealthy their comeuppance, and bring in a whole new social order. That did not happen and it has not happened yet. But something else did happen. Jesus was crucified and rose from the dead, and his disciples went out preaching that God had acted decisively. We can look at it like this:

If Jesus was 'the image of the invisible God', as Colossians puts it, or 'the Word, or wisdom, of God made flesh', as John's Gospel puts it, the crucifixion of Jesus shows us that God suffers, not just at one stage removed, like a sympathetic nurse, but as one of us.[8] God suffers, caught up in the network of injustices, self-interest and cruelties that are part of human society, and this network is taken into the life of God.

God's involvement in the life of the earth is not just in creative action and the giving of life, but also in suffering and death.[9] But death is not the last word. Out of the suffering and death God brings new life and possibilities, not just for the survivors, who can adjust to a new normal, but to those who have died. Dying is a part of the totality of life, and it is all a part of the life of God, so we can see death not as the end, but as a new beginning.

God is as God is in Jesus, not just Jesus dying on the cross and rising from the dead but Jesus teaching, healing, sharing meals, challenging the powerful, weeping with the mourners, and singing a song in the face of danger.[10] The Spirit or energy of God is continually at work as it was in Jesus.[11]

People can be empowered by the Spirit. A commitment to the concerns of God, whether it is in working for justice, or peace, or care for God's world, or in an explicit decision to be a follower of Jesus, brings a person into resonance with God. They are in tune with how things are meant to be, in harmony with God's music, going in God's direction. And the ultimate power is not with the systems and Powers, or with the exploiters and oppressors, but with God who brings life even out of death.

In and beyond time

We saw in chapter 10 how Jesus' message about the reign of God could be understood in a number of ways. It is described as being here and now; or to come at some unspecified time; or in a different but related or parallel realm. Within the history of the church all three possibilities have been championed. But perhaps these are not mutually exclusive alternatives. Perhaps they can be thought of as different emphases. In the book of Revelation Christ is described as 'the One who was, and is, and is to come'.[12]

Much depends on how we think about time and, of course, we do not know what time is or how it works. So far the biggest bestseller on the nature of time has been Stephen Hawking's *A Brief History of Time,* although shortly after it was published he reckoned he had got it wrong.[13] But if the cosmos with its basic structures of space, energy and time are God's creation, then God transcends time. All that is, all that has been, and all that will be could be considered present to God, although God is also involved in the cosmos and so acts within space and time.

This would mean that those like C.H. Dodd who believe that the reign of God is now; those like Ched Myers who see the reign of God as revolutionary change within society; those like Wolfhart Pannenberg who see it in the consummation of all things; and those like Kathryn Tanner who argue that the kingdom is beyond the world, all have a point.[14] As has been said of interfaith dialogue, it is often more helpful to understand what people affirm than what they deny. All the views have their limitations, but also their strengths.

If this is so, the reign of God can be seen in the compassion of people, in the many struggles for justice in the world, in the patient work of peacemaking where there is violence, and in all care for the damaged life of the earth. It can also be seen in the failures, rejections and suffering where God is continually crucified. And in the vision of how things might be.

God is also beyond the eternal now, not only in the struggle but also outside it, source of strength, imagination, life, love, and of new life beyond death. For the tired there is rest, because the struggle is not ultimately ours but God's. For the ground-down there is encouragement, because even in solitude we do not work alone. For those in darkness there is light, which one day we will see. And for those who die, there is new life.

Towards the end of the book of Revelation there is a vision of a removal of pain, grief and death in a process of renewal.[15] The cosmos is in process from its beginning in God towards a fulfilment in God. It is a process in which we are involved in our living and in our dying. And while we inevitably think of this in terms of a passage through time, because that is how we experience the world, the beginning and the end are beyond time. They are eternal.

Passionate concerns

But how? It is one thing to speak in metaphors like this about new life and so on. But how credible is it?

Firstly, we speak or write with metaphors because we have to. There are many ways of communicating and metaphor and myth are two of the most powerful and are used in the physical and social sciences as well as in poetry and theology.[16]

Secondly, it is not fundamentally a question of believing in resurrection or immortality, but of believing in God, in the sense of trusting God. In facing the prospect of death and disaster the challenge is not to try to understand what, if anything, we will experience. The challenge is to trust God.

Thirdly, we have our concerns for our society, and the future as it will affect people we care about. History teaches us that societies not only thrive but also collapse, sometimes in dire ways, and in the process people suffer. We cannot believe that any particular society has a God-given right to thrive when there is injustice, inhospitality, the abuse of power, and a disregard for truth and integrity. But change is always possible, and, again, the challenge is to trust God.

Fourthly, we are concerned for the life of the earth of which we are a part. Life will continue for some time to come although in the process many more species will become extinct, and, sooner or later, humanity will too. But there is so much about the living planet which many of us love. As I write this, signs of spring are visible from my window in the buds on the willow, the white blackthorn blossom in hedges, the primroses, daffodils, and celandines in different shades of yellow, and with the air ringing with the songs of blackbirds. I would love my grandchildren to be able to grow up to enjoy this when they are my age. I will do what I can to save it, but in the end, all I can do is trust God.

And that is the point about Jesus' declaration of the reign of God. It is God who is the ultimate power, the benefactor, and the life giver, not the imperial power, or the wheeler dealers, or the religious dignitaries, but God, as Jesus taught and showed God to be. God, in whom we live and move and have our being.[17] God who is concerned for the welfare of all creatures. God who loves, who suffers with the Creation, and through suffering and death, brings eternal life and renews hope.

Eternal creation

Various attempts have been made to explain how resurrection can work. Both Paul and the author of John's Gospel used an image of seeds dying and growing into new plants.[18] Paul also spoke about people having a 'spiritual body', although he did not explain what he actually meant.[19] The church, despite its creeds, was for centuries wedded to the Greek idea of an immortal soul embedded in a material body and released at death.[20] But what is a soul?

It is hard, if not impossible, to move beyond metaphors. And, as ever, some are useful and some come to the end of their life. We now know that if seeds actually die they do not produce a new plant. The concept of a soul is highly problematic. There is no way of knowing what death means for the person who has died. Studies of near-death experiences do not help much as, by definition, they are not experiences of death.

Nevertheless, there are perhaps some things we experience which can provide encouragement and images of life beyond death. One is of once-close personal relationships which have 'died', but then experienced new life.[21] Or an ecosystem which has seemed dead because of pollution or exploitation within a few years becoming a thriving lake or woodland. Or a once-thriving community shattered by violence and growing hatred not returning to its old form but becoming a new society, now enriched by memories which show what can happen without care and attention.

Most of us now write on a computer. The words we put on the screen are stored digitally and then transferred to another computer where they can be reproduced and read by someone else. What we have written remains even though it is now in totally different hardware and software.[22] There are few atoms in our bodies that were there ten years ago, yet we are each still the same person we were. We can look at old photos of ourselves and our friends as children and although our bodies have completely changed and they look very different, we can still recognise something of ourselves and them in the picture. Somehow, we retain our sense of identity despite our bodies being continually changed.

The hope of some New Testament writers was not just for individual resurrection but for a new creation.[23] The logic of this is that if the cosmos is God's creation, then God can make a new one. And in the same way that although we all have, literally, a different body now from the one we had as a child, what has been us, and others, and the whole living world, can be a part of that new creation.

Creation is talked about as a past event, and in a sense it is. What there was in the past was created. But so too is the present moment. Each moment is a time of creation.[24] It is also, as we pass from history into the future, a time of transition and of renewal. The suffering, death and resurrection of Jesus show this creative process is not brought to a halt by anything. Out of suffering and death God brings new life and possibilities. Or, as Saint Paul put it, 'Nothing can separate us from the love of God.'[25]

We can perhaps conceive of God at work within the various aspects of the world we are part of: within the randomness and patterns of matter, within life from single organisms to the great and complex mammals, within human society, and in the emotions and imaginations of individual people; continually calling it all into being with its structures, its limits and its freedoms. We can think of God as enjoying this creation, sharing its pleasure and also its pain, and drawing it through its pain and dying into new patterns and new life, both within and beyond time. And we can perhaps conceive of that because that is what we see when we look back or look around: that pattern of life, death and new life, from the stars to the sand on the shore, from the simplest to the most complex life we know, and in the life, death and resurrection of Jesus.

Hope now

It is many people's experience that being out in 'nature' gives them a sense of perspective or a feeling of hope, which others find through music, stories, art, or meditation. Seeing the world as a creation explains why: 'Nature' is God's work of art and the creativity of people is one way in which the energy of God continues to call new forms out of chaos. These can give a sense of hopefulness because they can put us in tune with the Creator who transcends the place and time in which we find ourselves.

There is no proof of this, and we can see the logic as circular. Thought and talk of God has arisen from experiences which have seemed to people to point them or even transport them beyond themselves. Over the centuries these ideas and words have been continually adapted and amended with new experiences, new ideas, and new challenges, but the ideas are fundamentally ways of interpreting the experiences.

From among the many interpretations that there are we have looked briefly at some themes of the Hebrew and Christian scriptures and tried to translate them into the view of the world we have in our own time. Significantly these scriptures claim to have arisen not only from interpretations of people's subjective experiences but also from things that they witnessed. We do not have access to those historical events and their interpretations are our principal sources but we can nevertheless conclude that behind their testimonies lie events such as the life, death and resurrection of Jesus. Our hope is thereby rooted not just in ideas but in our experience and in history.

My suggestion is that overall it makes sense to see the world in this way, as the creation of God beyond the world, within the world, suffering with it, and continually creating new life and possibilities within time and eternity. Our way of thinking about it will be continually amended in the light of new insights, and we can expect some of these to come from very different religious traditions, but this view can make sense of much that we experience and is a basis for hope. Finally, we need to think about what living with such hope might mean.

Part 5

LIVING

Chapter 17

Wisdom and hope

Word and wisdom

Writing is a strange business. Sometimes the words just flow but at other times it is a struggle to find the right word. Or the best word. The word that captures what you want to say and sits in the sentence giving the whole thing the sense and sentiment that you want to convey. Poets and songwriters will talk about how some lyrics simply come to them all at once and at other times they spend a long time trying one possibility after another. I wonder whether John, the traditional author of the fourth gospel, had that problem with the poem that begins the book.

'In the beginning was the Word, and the Word was God, and the Word was with God …' (John 1.1f). Of course, it echoes the poem at the beginning of Genesis, 'In the beginning God created the heavens and the earth …' (Genesis 1.1f). But why 'the Word'? The gospel was written in Greek and the word usually translated into English as 'Word', with a capital W, is *logos*. *Logos* means a word, like 'cat', 'dog' or 'kookaburra', but it also means communication, speech, teaching, reason, or self-expression, and it is from this Greek term that we get the English words biology, theology and logic. In Genesis God calls the world into existence, and God thereby expresses Godself.

But this introduction to the gospel does not just echo Genesis; it also refers to a poem in the heart of the book of Proverbs about wisdom. Wisdom is with God at the beginning, like a master-worker, creating and enjoying the world.[1] John is clearly suggesting that Jesus incarnates the wisdom of God, in which case why does he use the term Word, *logos*, rather than Wisdom, *sophia*?

The answer is probably that he is also referring to yet another strand in the Hebrew scriptures. Time and again they say 'The word of the Lord came to …' Samuel, Hosea, Zechariah, Malachi, or whoever.[2] When the word of the Lord came to them, they spoke on God's behalf and were thereby a prophet. A prophet was someone who spoke for God: someone who had a message or a 'word' from God. It might be a word of encouragement or of warning. It might take the form of a story or a poem, or be a simple blunt statement. But most importantly, it came from God, and it was usually a message for the present time.[3]

Now, what John is suggesting, is that the word of God is not only heard in words, poems, stories and proverbs, but in the whole life of this person, Jesus. God's wisdom is to be heard in his words and seen in his life. Jesus is both a teacher of wisdom and a prophet. More than that, in his life there are occasions when the creative word of God becomes particularly apparent: when hungry people are fed, an ill person is healed, or a dead man is given new life. But it is as if John is saying, 'Don't just listen to what he says, or even look at the remarkable things he does, but see his whole life, death and resurrection and you will see something of God.'[4]

Missing the point

This opening passage is fundamental to the whole gospel. If it is ignored, and especially if John's Gospel is taken on its own, it gives a very distorted view of Jesus and what he was about. John's Gospel contains few parables or proverbs. The teaching of Jesus which Matthew gives in the Sermon on the Mount[5] is not included, neither are the great parables of the Prodigal Son and the Good Samaritan which Luke includes,[6] or the stories of the Sower, the Mustard Seed, and the Weeds.[7] What John has is long speeches from Jesus, largely about who he is: a source of living water, the bread of life, the true vine, the light of the world, the good shepherd, the way, the truth and the life.[8]

Seen as reflections on the significance of Jesus, whose teaching and character are known from the other gospels, such statements make some sense. Taken in isolation they appear to be signs of a severe personality disorder,[9] or the words of someone who is not actually human. Sadly, that has often happened in the church: Jesus has come to be seen not as a man but as something else.[10]

It has also led to exclusiveness. If Jesus is seen as the incarnation of the creative word and wisdom of God then a statement such as 'No one comes to the Father but by me' (John 14.6) suggests that whoever comes to God is drawn there by God's wisdom, whatever their religion or world view. But if that introductory poem is ignored it easily comes to suggest that only people who can talk about and pray to Jesus can come to God. This distorted and exclusive view has been widely held and has inevitably led to bad relations between Christians and people of other religions.[11]

Working it out

Down the centuries Jesus has been seen in many different ways and different groups have championed him as their own: gun-toting red-necks and woke pacifists, Marxist community workers and financial traders. At the time of the Reformation the cry was that church teachers needed to go back to the sources because their idea of what Jesus was about had become so distorted that a reset was needed. The source for seeing what Jesus was about is the gospels. Ignore the gospels and anyone can imagine a Jesus to fit their own aspirations and lifestyle. The gospels are a reference point: they are like lenses through which Jesus, the wise man, prophet, healer and teacher from Nazareth, is seen.

Jesus was not a stand-alone figure: he belonged within the Jewish tradition and, according to Matthew, saw himself as completing rather than doing away with the Torah.[12] The Commandments condemn covetousness but Jesus takes this further and says, 'You cannot serve God and wealth.'[13] The Commandments condemn false witness[14] but Jesus says, 'Let your Yes be Yes and your No be No.'[15] Jesus condemns Pharisees who use a theoretical dedication of their wealth to God to avoid their social responsibility in looking after their aging parents.[16]

While the Commandments have an instruction about respecting parents, who may still have some wisdom to impart, they say nothing about respecting children. But concern for future generations is given as the reason for keeping the Commandments in the first place.[17] With no view of or concern about an afterlife the continuation of the family and society were high priorities. Jesus strengthened the case and taught that children were valuable not only as the future but in themselves now, as they were loved by and represented God.[18]

We live in a society which values children in some ways but at the same time fails to care about the world they will live in. However, there are many people, groups and organisations which are working and campaigning to counter this prevailing culture which is causing the ecological crisis. They come from a range of backgrounds and societies, many simply responding to a gut concern for the world and future generations, while others are explicitly working from a religious or philosophical base. Whatever their background they can be seen as responding to the One Creator.[19]

Words and deeds

John's Gospel suggests that it is not only the words of Jesus that matter but the whole life. Jesus was not just a teacher but wisdom personified. He was not just a preacher: his whole life was a demonstration of the grace of God. Jesus shows what God is like, and that God is not beyond the mess of the world but involved in it. God does not wave a hand and make things OK but goes with us through suffering and death to new life.

The wisdom that Jesus taught and lived, and which we can access through the gospels, does not cover all eventualities. It did not directly relate to every issue even of his own time. He was not an agony uncle or a counsellor. People had to work out for themselves or with others what they were to do, and the early Christian letters show people doing just that. Over the following centuries this has continued within the Christian movement. There have been agreements, and many disagreements.[20] The debate which runs through the Hebrew scriptures continued into the New Testament and continues now. But if Jesus is seen as the Word and Wisdom of God then he is a reference point. We can expect there to be disagreement but not every view is going to be valid and we can check out our positions against Jesus' teaching, example, and life story.

John also has Jesus promising his disciples that the Spirit will guide them.[21] People have sometimes claimed, and continue to claim, that they are led or guided by the Spirit. This happened early on in the church and the test was not how wild, extreme or erudite the person was, but whether what they said and did was in accord with what was known about Jesus. Jesus was the touchstone against which their visions, pronouncements or actions were to be checked.[22]

Healing energy

Jesus in the gospels is not only a teacher of wisdom and a prophet, but also a healer. We considered in chapter 3 some reasons why it is not wise to place too much hope on those who have power within our society. But it is worth thinking briefly again about those reasons and seeing how the message and actions of Jesus relate to them. The first point was that people are people, and those with power, wealth or celebrity status are no different from everyone else. This reflects Jesus' attitude, with his appreciation of and concern for people who were pushed to the edges of society: the beggars, lepers, and desperately poor. The slogan 'God loves losers' might sum that up.

We thought too about how we are more complex than we sometimes first appear. We are all shaped by both our genes and our environment, and we have deep-seated and often unconscious drives, fears and emotional wounds. Over the last hundred years there has been not only a growing understanding of these but many different ways have developed of helping and sometimes healing people. Whether or not the people developing these have had a clear sense of and faith in God, improved understanding and therapies can be seen, like other medical insights and practice, as the work of God's healing spirit which was seen in Jesus.[23]

Our childhood memories and experiences stay with us and continue to influence our lives. Jesus frequently spoke about God as a loving parent and some religious and spiritual practices enable participants to enter into a childlike mode of being for a short while. Jesus spoke about the need to enter the reign of God like a child: trusting and inquisitive. It has been suggested that the normal cycle of a Christian service can facilitate this in a constructive way as it gives participants a chance to step out of their normal responsibilities and roles and simply accept that they are valued as they are: with their doubts, anxieties, failures, and successes.[24] They can then step back into the fray of normal life with new energy. There are no doubt many other practices which have the same result.

We thought too about how ideological filters can lead to unhelpful or even destructive decisions being made. Seeing the wisdom of God in the person of Jesus, who is known through the gospels, enables a critique of dominant value systems. Taking the scriptures not as a unified theory or theology but as a continuing debate provides insights for continually relativising what might otherwise become all-embracing. Within the last century a great deal of this sort of work has been done in many different situations, from the German Confessing Church to liberation theology, and from the American Civil Rights Movement to Sabeel in Jerusalem and Dalit theology in India.[25] In such activities God undermines the illusions and pretensions of those who hold power through the ballot box, the media, or the gun.

But as we have also noted, power is not just with individuals but also in impersonal systems: what Walter Wink called 'the Powers'. It has always been so, and dominating powers have often been challenged in the name of the creative and loving God. Successful challenges have often not been direct confrontations, which can sometimes mean simply exchanging one dominating system for another, but oblique criticisms through humour, peaceful demonstrations and art, or simply by people adopting a different lifestyle and so calling out the Powers for what they are.[26]

Strategy and grace

Jesus was not naive and did not want his followers to be. Reading between the lines of the synoptic gospels it seems that Jesus decided when to begin his preaching, and his teaching was either brilliant extemporising or carefully crafted. Perhaps it was both. He did not wander aimlessly around but chose where to go, and avoided cities such as Tiberias and Sepphoris. He tried to pace himself and to take breaks, and when he went to Jerusalem he timed it beautifully. Arriving during the Passover was no accident and he had clearly made some preparations, such as the provision of a donkey and a room for the Passover meal.[27]

He told his disciples that they must be 'wise as serpents and innocent as doves'.[28] One of the criticisms made of Christian activists is that they are sometimes naive. We thought in chapter 3 about how Reinhold

Niebuhr criticised the Social Gospel movement in his time for its lack of understanding about power. The wisdom of serpents is needed for real social change and acting with it sometimes involves getting mucky. Dietrich Bonhoeffer criticised Christians during the Nazi dictatorship who wanted to keep their hands clean, and told them that was not an option when the times were evil.[29] The answer was not purity but grace.

As we have seen, choices are often not between a good and a bad but between two bads, and sometimes failing to act simply allows evil to continue or even to grow. In such cases what is needed to is to act, not necessarily claiming to be doing good but acknowledging that while what we are doing is wrong the alternative seems even worse.[30] This brings us back to a fundamental aspect of Jesus' life and teaching, which is that God is gracious and forgives.

As we have seen, this is a thread running through the Hebrew scriptures and when Jesus criticised the scribes and Pharisees for their lack of grace he was simply reminding them of this. It lies behind the Torah and is a major theme of the Prophets, the Psalms and the wisdom writings. We are called to trust in the grace of God for our life now and for the future.

Real power

The prognosis is not good for our global society. It is destroying the planet's complex ecosystems and changing the climate. It has vast stores of weapons of mass destruction. While some people have more wealth than they can use, others starve. Millions live in camps and shanties while others defend their property and privileges with rhetoric, laws or violence. A few people have enormous power and influence; many have little say in what will happen to them. We could go on but any one of those aspects of our society can be deemed as foolish, or worse.

In our search for wisdom we have looked at the Hebrew and Christian scriptures. Many of their writers would see our behaviour as more than foolish. We saw how at the heart of the Torah are commands to not covet, and to speak truth, but covetousness and misinformation are fundamental to our consumer society. The Commandments begin with the instruction to honour God but our society, however it might use the word 'God', has little respect for the concerns and values of God as described in the Torah and the Prophets.

The tales recounted in these books and the picture that emerges from modern historical study all point out that civilisations, states and empires come and go. None is too big to fail. The prophets' demands for justice within society carry as their corollary that societies that lack justice will fail.

Often the prophets also said that a society that radically changed might survive. Radical change is often translated as 'repentance', which is not about feeling bad but living differently. Perhaps there will be radical change in our culture. Some commentators think that it is too late to avert catastrophe, while others reckon that change is still possible and we could enter into an era of true sustainability.[31] We do not know what will happen.

There continue to be people who pore over the books of the Bible hoping to find out what will happen. But the fantasies of Revelation, rich though they might be in messages of encouragement and warning, are not going to tell us the future any more than the myths of Genesis tell us what actually happened. That is not what they are for. The future is not like a script which will play itself out; it is shaped by the choices and actions of humans and other creatures.

What Jesus points to in the gospels is that beyond and within that process is God, and that the ultimate power is God's. The emperors of the world, the presidents and prime ministers, the CEOs of vast corporations, the financial dealers and those with great wealth might flatter themselves that they are in control and have the resources to avoid disaster but it is not so. The One who is glimpsed in the vastness of space and the beauty of a living forest, who suffers with the hungry and the stateless, who works through the compassion and skills of those who attend to other people's needs, and who builds communities and heals social wounds is One who brings new life out of death. And so we can hope even in the face of great uncertainty.

Chapter 18

Living hope

Hope is not just an idea; neither is it a feeling. It is an attitude or an orientation. It is a way of living. The basis of hope is God, and living with hope is a matter of trusting God. Not a god that is going to break in and make everything OK, or unmake the bad that has happened, but God beyond and within time and matter, continually calling it into existence and working within it to create new life and new possibilities. We are concerned about the life of this planet Earth. We are concerned about our society and where it is heading. We are concerned for people we know, and for the many we do not know who are caught up in wars, impoverished, enslaved, abused, or suffering from earthquakes, mudslides, floods and droughts. So is God and when we do what we can to ease the suffering, to make peace where there is violence and justice where there is oppression, to speak truth amidst lies, and to bring healing where there is disease, we are in tune with the creative love of God. The energy or Spirit of God flows through us.

When we ourselves are crippled by circumstances, or pain, or despair, we not separated from God. God is with us and somehow will bring us through it. The picture we have of God is Jesus of Nazareth, the healer who is crucified and risen. That is why he is called the Word of God, and the Son of God. And he is called the Christ or Messiah because he brings the reign of God through his life, death, resurrection, and new life.

Stopping

At times of pressure, when the demands were heavy, Jesus told his disciples to come with him and take a break. Sometimes he would go off on his own and pray. It is tempting when there is so much to do to rush straight into action, but all religious traditions speak of the importance of meditation, contemplation, prayer, or reflection. These are, or can be, ways of recharging our energy, clarifying our vision, or working out our priorities. There is so much to do and we cannot do everything.

We may not be able to do much. But our hope and the hope of the Creation is not based on our actions but on God. We can stop sometimes, and we need to.

So living hope is going to involve meditation, or prayer, or whatever we call this kind of activity. And the earth that we are concerned about can be our starting point. Many people's experience is that being out in the open air, able to see trees or grass, flowers, birds, or flowing water is helpful and energising. Yes, these are often damaged and polluted, but the glory is still there and might be seen breaking through. Stopping, looking and paying attention is helpful and can be a way of being in the moment rather than in an imagined future or remembered past. The past is over and many possible future events never happen. As well as looking, or listening, it is valuable to feel. Turning soil with our hands, feeling the wind or rain on our face, kneading bread or shaping wood can all help us know through our senses that we are a part of the world. We are not detached from the world. We are not disembodied minds. We are a small part of the whole.[1]

Thinking and feeling

Nevertheless, we do have minds and we can use them to explore, to understand more, and to try to make sense of what is happening. Sometimes we can be so concerned with the big picture that we miss what is happening in the detail, and so not allow ourselves to be intrigued, amused, or awestruck by what is going on around us. At other times we need to look at the big picture, and be encouraged or energised by that. It is possible to be so continually moved by news of ecological disasters that we can miss some of the big trends for positive change. Sometimes things are not as bad as the continual headlines might lead us to feel.[2] And there are also some significant shifts in attitude and ways of thinking taking place.[3]

However, sometimes and in some ways things really are bad: bad for us or for other people, for the forests, the oceans, the insects, the birds. Our imaginations draw us into feeling compassion for these creatures, and our imaginations can help us cope. We can perhaps imagine, in the middle of it, Jesus despairing and being crucified in the darkness. Or, if we cannot do that, maybe we can use someone else's imagining by looking at a crucifix, or a picture. From time to time, we need things to remind us that despite our sense of bereavement and loss, God is in the world and is the One who suffers. In our imaginations we can stay there in the darkness. This is how the world is and it does not help to pretend otherwise.

It is important not to ignore this grief. In the Hebrew scriptures there are psalms and poems of lamentation.[4] This is a spiritual tradition which the church is now rediscovering.[5] There is value in acknowledging the pain of life and the distress of the world not just with our minds but with our emotions.

Of course, that is not all there is. God not only suffers, God creates. Jesus does not just die, he is raised from the dead. There is not just darkness, there is also light. But they come in their own time; or in God's time. To move too fast through grief is to trivialise the suffering. It is like well-meaning people who to try to find silver linings in other people's clouds when they would do better to help them acknowledge their pain.

Music can help with this. It can resonate with our mood, be it classical, rock, blues, or whatever. Music can sometimes resonate with our deep emotions and in so doing speak for us. It can be a kind of prayer without words, which is not asking or pleading but simply being there in the pain with God and sometimes with other people. With music, poetry or visual art help can sometimes come through our realising that someone else feels or felt as we do. We are not alone. And sometimes our companions, who speak for us or catch our mood in their art, are people of a very different place or time. Art can bring people together and bridge great gulfs.

Sometimes we need to make a point of meeting with other people, whether we feel like it or not. There are people who try to fix our problems with sticking-plaster solutions, or cheer us up with jokes or with stories about themselves, but many do not. And people who can let us be ourselves are a great help. They are channels of the Spirit of God who accepts us as we are. God does not expect us to snap out of our grief or sadness but walks with us through it.[6]

Celebration

Then there does come a time for celebration because, despite the mess, the world is beautiful. Despite the greed and violence many people do care about each other. From situations of disaster come numerous stories of people putting themselves out and working to help each other. It is important to hear of these things, and to allow ourselves to wonder at the world and the life we are part of.

It is also important to join this work of healing, caring, peace-making, and pursuing justice. Jesus took his disciples to lonely places occasionally but in order that, refreshed, they could return to the work. There is much to do. We cannot do it all, but we have our part within the whole drama of the Spirit, and our part is not someone else's part. We have our own skills, personalities, gifts and opportunities. We all have different experiences and insights. What we are called to do is particular to us.

For some of us it is local and low key: speaking to neighbours, greeting strangers, feeding birds, picking up litter. For some it is local politics or community-building, counselling, joining or organising demonstrations, writing to representatives, guerrilla gardening, involvement in a local wildlife reserve, helping at a food bank, or supporting other people or organisations who are able to do what we cannot. For some people their calling is working in business or a union, national politics, high-profile campaigning, research, podcasting, teaching, or journalism.

What we can do at one point in our lives we may not be able to do at another. We are called to do what we can when we can: not to save the world but to join with what God is doing in it and for it.

With others

In the gospels Jesus never has just one disciple. From the beginning of his preaching and teaching he has two or three people he has invited to join him. Then a lot more come along, twelve of whom he chooses to be his representatives and calls 'apostles', or ambassadors. Sometimes there are seventy or more also doing the work and large crowds gather to hear what he has to say and to ask for his help. It goes on from there. After his resurrection there are several hundred of them in Jerusalem and the movement grows, first among Jews and then others join in as well.

That was the beginning of the church two thousand years ago and a lot has happened in the meantime. Basically, the word 'church' means the people who take Jesus seriously: people who are, metaphorically, 'followers' of Jesus. Over time the movement got itself organised in various ways; there were major disruptions, reorganisations and splits. The word 'church' has now come to mean many things: the whole Christian movement, one of the organisations within it, the dominant one in a particular place, or a building.

It is possible to talk at length about the appalling things that church organisations and rogue Christians have done down the years; as well as about how in some parts of the world the churches are growing, while in others they have the appearance of relics from another age; and also about the many ways that churches or their members have worked, and continue to work, to relieve suffering, create peace, and campaign for justice. Much of that is well documented in numerous histories of the church and of the world, and information about current activity can be found through the websites of such organisations as Christian Aid, CAFOD, the Iona Community, and many others.[7]

We also have to acknowledge that without the church we could not have explored the question of hope in the way we have: the transmission, translation and analysis of the scriptures we have used have all been the work of the church in one way or another.

The church, whichever way we take that word, can be a valuable resource. The Bible is a product of the church and can be a source of wisdom. The gospels and other writings are the windows through which we can see the person of Jesus. Meetings of Christians can be an encouragement or a stimulus to action. Christian communities can live and demonstrate God's values. Groups of Christians can act together for change. The insights of scholars and other Christians can help us think and church members who have explored different paths of spirituality can help us to meditate, pray, listen, and sing. Church buildings can be used in many ways and the worship of the church can give a sense of the Transcendent, or at least a reminder that there is more to life than the mundane.

When they point beyond themselves to God the churches can help engender the hope we need, as can other organisations and communities. The Celtic blessing with which I began this book was thought to come from the Iona Community, which has been a great help to me, as have some other groups such as Green Christian, together with numerous writers and broadcasters, course leaders and teachers in organised gatherings and in random discussions. So too have numerous people who in spontaneous conversations sent my thinking in a new direction or helped me make new connections.

All these are invaluable. We cannot manage on our own. But ultimately the basis of our hope is not the church or any other organisation, neither is it any person, economic system, political programme, or state. Our hope is in God who is beyond and within it all.

Action

There is a story in the Hebrew scriptures about the prophet Elijah who felt that he was fighting for a lost cause and despaired. He set off to curl up and die on the Mountain of God. When he got there he went into a cave and after a while a great fire swept past the cave. Then there was an earthquake, and then a great wind. After the wind there was silence, and God spoke to him in the silence. God asked him what he was doing there and Elijah told God he was the only one left who was faithful to God so it was hopeless and he wanted to die. God did not blame Elijah for his despair but told him to go and get on with a particular job, and also told him that there were actually thousands of people who were still faithful. Elijah left and did as he was told.[8]

In any number of fields there are new insights and initiatives. It remains to be seen whether we will move into a sustainable way of living with an economy and politics that values the earth and all people, but we cannot give up simply because we cannot see whether or not we are going to make it. The earth and other people need us to do what we can, and the source of wisdom which gives us reason to hope can also give us some guidance as to how to live sustainably. I will make a few tentative suggestions as examples of the kind of thing we might find if we look.

Jesus' teaching about creative non-violence is applicable to many situations.[9] Perhaps it is also applicable in the situation of soft oppression which is the experience of many people in Western society. Big companies, advertisers and moneylenders persuade people to spend money they do not have on things they do not want or need, and are trashing the planet in the process. Perhaps this can be challenged with the kind of fortitude, creativity and humour which non-violence uses. It calls for creative thinking but – why not?

Jesus was quite blunt about it: 'You cannot serve God and wealth' (Matthew 6.24). 'Do not lay up treasure on earth … but lay up your treasure in heaven …' (Matthew 6.19–21). For centuries that was interpreted as needing to be concerned about an afterlife rather than this one, and that helped the rich and powerful keep the poor from rebelling.[10] But if 'heaven' is not an afterlife but is the reign of God, and that includes God's activity now, then 'laying up treasure in heaven' will mean using our resources for God's concerns. As Jesus also said, when he was telling his disciples not to be anxious, 'Look first for the reign of God and his justice, and what you need will be yours' (Matthew 6.33, my paraphrase).

There is more in the gospels and in the other scriptures about money. The writers had a very different economic system from ours and although ours has long been seen as superior, our system of consumer capitalism is not working; in fact, it is destroying the life systems in which it is enmeshed. There are other ways of doing things and we would do well to see how they measure up to the wisdom of the Hebrew and Christian scriptures. For example, the model of 'Doughnut Economics' proposed by Kate Raworth seems to fit well with the insight of us humans being a part of the life of the world; and its recommendation of working for human flourishing rather than the accumulation of wealth fits better with the values of the reign of God.[11]

In the same way that there are different ways of organising an economy, so too there are many ways of structuring and choosing a government. Democracy is based on the principle that every person has value and should be able to contribute to the whole community, including in choosing its leaders. Jesus' idea of leadership was that it was to serve, and he exemplified this in his concern for the good of everyone, and particularly those who had little power in their society, be it through poverty, status, or disability.[12] A basic question to ask of those who wish to have the power and responsibility of government is whether they value everyone and are concerned to work for the good of all, and especially those who themselves have little agency.

We could go on and consider issues about truth and honesty, about the value of children, about land, food, justice, and freedom, but the point is that our present economic and political systems are not working and all life on the planet is in danger. Significant change is needed urgently. We need new ways of doing things, and in developing these we can learn from past societies and their wisdom. Among others, the people who wrote the Hebrew and Christian scriptures have much to teach us.[13]

Significant change will not be easy. Those who benefit from the exploitation of other people and of the earth will not readily give up their power and privilege. But no one in the scriptures said that living in tune with the Creator God was going to be easy. The words of Moses to the Israelites as they were about to enter their new land are also apt for us: 'I call heaven and earth to witness against you today that I have set before you life and death, blessings and curses. Choose life so that you and your descendants may live' (Deuteronomy 30.19). And to Moses' successor, Joshua, God said, 'I hereby command you: be strong and courageous; do not be frightened or dismayed, for Yahweh your God is with you wherever you go' (Joshua 1.9).

God: not a superbeing armed with a flaming sword, thunderbolts, or sticking plaster, but the Mystery beyond and within all that is; who calls the cosmos into being and loves the Creation; who enjoys its beauty and suffers its pain; and who brings it through death into new life and possibilities. And so we hope.[14]

Sunrise: A poem

Soft fading stars above a misted meadow,
slow waking dawn of colour painting light,
a thrush's song, the fox's silent footsteps,
the rising day, the buzzard's curving flight
declare your glory
bursting through life's wonders;
Creator God,
within, beyond all plans:
help us to see your life in each day's tapestry,
help us to walk this world as through your land.

Teacher who sees God's kingdom in life's trials,
a friend of children, prostitutes and cheats,
healer who feels the anguish in a beggar's voice
and weeps for blinded guides who will not see;
nailed up in glory,
bursting through death's prison door;
Lord Jesus Christ,
God's grace among us here:
help us to see your face in every neighbour
and live with you the love that casts out fear.

Slow dance of love that weaves life out of chaos,
strong wind of hope across our storm-turned seas,
music of friendship, laughter, tears and silence,
deep power of joy that sets earth's children free:
lift up to glory
those who seek your justice,
bring to your morning
those who yearn for light;
Spirit of God, help us to hear your playing
and make heaven's song the measure of earth's life.

Tune: Can be sung to *Londonderry Air*, aka *Danny Boy*.

Suggestions for further reading

For most of us our first port of call to find out about something is the Internet. It is a wonderful resource with more information than we could possibly want but it does have drawbacks. It contains not only valuable information and wisdom but also bigotry and downright lies so the difficulty is not so much finding information but judging how reliable it is. The information also comes to us in the order of our searching and sometimes it is helpful to have someone else shape it up for us with a developed argument or presentation. Books can do this and be more fun and relaxing, whether we read them on a screen or on old-fashioned paper.

The notes for each chapter of this book give some of my sources. They also suggest books, and occasionally websites, which give more detailed information or argument than I have been able to provide. And below are some books that I particularly recommend. They are all written for general readers rather than specialists; for people who just want to find out more and to think things over, rather than for academic research.

If you want to know more about the authors, consult Wikipedia, which is generally reliable in such matters.

Science

Some TV programmes, such as those presented by Jim Al-Khalili, Brian Cox, David Attenborough or Chris Packham, are not only entertaining but also informative and accurate. There is also often an accompanying book.

In addition to those, I recommend the Oxford University Press series of *Very Short Introductions* which include many aspects of science as well as philosophy and history.

Also:

Bill Bryson, *A Short History of Nearly Everything*, Doubleday, 2003.
For those who think they know next to nothing about science, this is an excellent, readable, and entertaining introduction.

Martin Rees, *Just Six Numbers: The Deep Forces that Shape the Universe*, Weidenfeld and Nicholson, 1999.
A mind-blowing but clear explanation by a leading astronomer of how the Big Bang, black holes, multiverses, dark matter, and all the rest are linked.

Carlo Rovelli, *The Order of Time,* Penguin, 2019.
A playful, poetic, and fun exploration by a theoretical physicist of one of the great mysteries.

Ian Stewart, *Nature's Numbers: Discovering Order and Pattern in the Universe*, Weidenfeld & Nicolson, 1995.
A mathematician explains unsuspected structures and regularities in the world around us.

Understanding religious experience

John Hick, *The Fifth Dimension: An Exploration of the Spiritual Realm*, Oneworld, 2004.
A renowned philosopher of religion presents a strong case for taking religious experience and spirituality seriously.

Marcus Borg, *Days of Awe and Wonder*, SPCK, 2017.
A posthumous collection of papers by a New Testament scholar which includes his account of his realisation that religious experience and not just ideas should be taken seriously.

Peter Berger, *A Rumour of Angels: Modern Society and the Rediscovery of the Supernatural,* Penguin, 1969.
The 'supernatural' of the subtitle is not spooks and zombies but the Transcendent, which Berger argues is part of our everyday experience. A classic.

David Hay, *Religious Experience Today: Studying the Facts,* Mowbray, 1990, or *Exploring Inner Space: Is God Still Possible in the Twentieth Century?* Mowbray, 1987.
Information and conclusions from research into religious experience by the Director of the Alister Hardy Research Centre in Oxford.

Religion, science and culture

Karen Armstrong, *The Case for God: What Religion Really Means*, The Bodley Head, 2009.
Not what you might expect from the title but a history of religion, philosophy, theology, and science from the Stone Age to postmodernism, brilliantly told.

Paul Tillich, *Theology of Culture*, Oxford University Press, 1959.
Essays by one of the great philosophical theologians of the twentieth century on subjects such as religion as a dimension of life, religious language, and science and theology.

Walter Wink, *The Powers That Be: Theology for a New Millennium*, Doubleday, 1998.
This is a digest of a trilogy of books, known as *The Powers Series*, in which the author interprets the state of the world as a field of competing systems which are principally characterised by domination and violence, and suggests how we can engage with them.

Hebrew and Christian scriptures: The texts

There are numerous translations of these books, usually collected together under the title The Bible, or The Holy Bible. Any translation is a work of interpretation as many phrases and words can mean several different things. Translators bring to their work their own overarching way of seeing the world, and what they think the texts are likely to say. They are also interpreting the text with a particular readership in mind.

So it is that some modern translations of the Bible, like the very popular *The Message*, are quite overtly a retelling of the story, while others, like the *New Revised Standard Version* (NRSV) or the *Revised English Bible* (REB), aim at accuracy rather than ease of reading.

I recommend these latter two translations which are the work of teams of scholars with a broad range of outlooks, and are recommended by the mainstream Churches in countries where English is the main language.

Hebrew and Christian scriptures: Background

For introductions to the social and historical background of the Bible the writings of John Drane are very helpful and come well presented with illustrations. See particularly:
John Drane, *The World of the Bible*, Lion, 2009; *Introducing the Old Testament*, 3rd Edition, Lion, 2011; *Introducing the New Testament*, 4th Edition, Lion, 2019.

Walter Brueggemann, *The Prophetic Imagination*, 2nd Edition, Fortress Press, 2001.
The renowned scholar sees the Old and New Testaments as directly relevant to the crises of power and consumption in our present society, and argues his case clearly.

Geza Vermes, *Jesus in His Jewish Context*, SCM, 2003.
Vermes had his cultural roots in both Roman Catholicism and Judaism, and became a specialist in the Judaism of the time of Jesus and Jesus' place within it.

E.P. Sanders, *The Historical Figure of Jesus*, Penguin, 1993.
Ed Sanders was a major figure in the late twentieth-century exploration of the history of Jesus and the origins of Christianity. This book is an excellent introduction.

Bruce J. Malina, *The New Testament World: Insights from Cultural Anthropology*, SCM, 1983.
One of the first of many recent books considering the Christian scriptures from a social scientific background: an approach which has brought many fascinating and helpful insights.

Gerd Theissen, *The Shadow of the Galilean*, SCM, 2001.
A novel by an expert in the cultural and historical context of the gospels which accurately conveys how the activity of Jesus might have come across to people of the time.

Hebrew and Christian scriptures: Commentaries

Even more than translations, commentaries on texts vary considerably depending on the outlook, methods, assumptions, and beliefs of the writer. They also differ in how detailed they are. For a one-volume commentary on the whole Bible I recommend:

John Muddiman and John Barton, editors, *The Oxford Bible Commentary*, Oxford University Press, 2001.
It is a whopping doorstep of a book but is also accessible online. It includes background information on each book and a section-by-section commentary by a team of more than seventy international scholars on every book in the Old and New Testaments, and the Apocrypha.

Claus Westermann, *Creation*, SPCK and Fortress, 1974.
This book has been around for a long time now but is a very accessible commentary on the opening chapters of Genesis by a great Old Testament scholar. It is particularly helpful for anyone who has suffered from literal readings of the creation stories and wants to see beyond them.

John D. Davies, *Beginning Now: Contemporary Experience of Creation and Fall*, Collins, 1971, and *God at Work: Creation Then and Now – A Practical Exploration*, Canterbury Press, 2001.
Accessible but also deep readings of the texts of Genesis 1–3, always with an eye to the practical implications.

Bruce J. Malina and Richard L. Rohrbaugh, *Social Science Commentary on the Synoptic Gospels*, Fortress, 1992.
This applies the insights of cultural anthropology to an examination of Matthew, Mark and Luke, with fascinating and enlightening results.

Theology

Alister McGrath, *Christian Theology: An Introduction*, Blackwell, 6th Edition, 2016.
Comprehensive, very readable, and easy to dip into, this book gives a historical introduction to the development of Christian theology and summarises the main themes. The author has doctorates in molecular biophysics, theology, and intellectual history, and writes clearly. His

books on science and theology are also worth looking out for.

John V. Taylor, *The Christlike God*, SCM, 1992.
A rich and gently argued challenge to many traditional ideas about God by a former Bishop of Winchester. His other writings include *Enough is Enough*, SCM, 1973, which is a strong criticism of consumerism, and *The Go-Between God*, SCM, 1972, a prize-winning study of the Holy Spirit as the energy of God in the world.

Elizabeth A. Johnson, *She Who Is: The Mystery of God in Feminist Theological Discourse*, Crossroad, 2002.
A groundbreaking book by a Catholic theologian. It has now become a classic, bringing a feminist perspective to discussions which have in the past been dominated by men.

W.H. Vanstone, *Love's Endeavour, Love's Expense: The Response of Being to the Love of God*, Darton, Longman & Todd, 1977.
A prize-winning masterpiece and now a classic, by a vicar who was also no mean scholar.

James P. Mackey, *Christianity and Creation: The Essence of the Christian Faith and Its Future among the Religions*, Continuum, 2006.
A hugely positive final work from a systematic theologian and philosopher which takes seriously the mythical and poetical character of the Bible and much traditional theology.

Richard Bauckham & Trevor Hart, *Hope Against Hope: Christian Eschatology in Contemporary Context*, Darton, Longman & Todd, 1999.
This considers the ways that secular hope has failed and assesses some of the Christian models of hope that have been held in the past and continue to be held today.

Engaging theology and science

John Polkinghorne, *Science and Creation: The Search for Understanding*, SPCK, 1988.
One of several books in which the writer, who was both a theoretical physicist and an Anglican priest, makes connections between scientific and theological insights.

Ian Barbour, *Myths, Models and Paradigms*, SCM, 1974.
A scientist and theologian, Barbour looks at how scientific and religious thinking works, and notes the similarities and differences. Particularly significant is the notion of paradigm shifts which happen in both disciplines.

Ian Barbour, *Nature, Human Nature and God*, SPCK, 2002.
Barbour challenges reductionism and engages science and theology with a range of subjects, including genetics, AI, and environmental justice.

Jürgen Moltmann, *Science and Wisdom*, SCM, 2003.
A collection of papers and lectures on such issues as scientific method, the nature of the universe, biomedical ethics, and the future.

Ruth Page, *God and the Web of Creation*, SCM, 1996.
A theologian's vision of God involved in and suffering with the world in crisis.

Celia Deane-Drummond, *Wonder and Wisdom: Conversations in Science, Spirituality and Theology*, Darton, Longman & Todd, 2006.
A Professor of Theology and Biological Sciences draws on and relates both fields of study with profound implications for life as a whole.

David Hutchings and David Wilkinson, *God, Stephen Hawking and the Multiverse: What Hawking Said and Why It Matters*, SPCK, 2020.
A very readable introduction to Hawking's cosmology and an exploration of how this relates to theology.

Living with hope

Brian McLaren, *Life after Doom: Wisdom and Courage for a World Falling Apart*, Hodder & Stoughton, 2024.
McLaren takes the reader through a process of confronting the evidence of what is happening to the Earth and the possible future scenarios, facing up to and owning our feelings about it, and then perhaps discovering a new joyful energy for taking what action we can.

Hannah Ritchie, *Not the End of the World: Surprising Facts, Dangerous Myths and Hopeful Solutions for our Future on Planet Earth*, Penguin, 2024.

A data scientist takes a broad and long view of what is happening on the planet and concludes that all is not yet lost and there are some exciting things going on.

Kate Raworth, *Doughnut Economics: Seven Ways to Think Like a 21st-Century Economist*, Penguin, 2017.
Raworth presents a challenge to unsustainable business-as-usual economic thinking and presents an alternative model which will enable life on the planet to thrive. This bigger and deeper approach is now gaining traction.

David Osborne, *Love for the Future: A Journey*, Wild Goose Publications, 2013.
My reflections during a pilgrimage to Iona suggest spiritual practices which can help us become better able to respond with creativity, hope and love to the challenges of the ecological crisis.

Jürgen Moltmann, *Ethics of Hope*, SCM, 2012.
Theologian Jürgen Moltmann has always been concerned about and engaged with the social, ethical and political issues of the time. Here he draws out explicitly some of the implications for how we are to live and act, particularly in the fields of medicine, ecology, and violence, war and peacemaking.

Jürgen Moltmann, *In the End – the Beginning*, SCM, 2004.
Here Moltmann writes in an accessible way on issues of suffering, mortality, and the crises of our time.

Walter Brueggemann, editor, *Hope for the World: Mission in a Global Context*, Westminster John Knox Press, 2001.
Writers from various parts of the world point to the profound implications for society of Christian hope.

Marcus J. Borg, *The Heart of Christianity: Rediscovering a Life of Faith*, Harper Collins, 2003.
Borg sees a contrast between traditional and progressive Christianity and argues that the latter is both true to Christian origins and to the compassion and Spirit of God. Borg's expected readership is his fellow

Americans but what he says is relevant to questioning Christians wherever they are.

Richard Rohr, *Simplicity: The Freedom of Letting Go*, Crossroad, 2003.
One of a number of collections of talks and occasional writings by the founder of the Center for Action and Contemplation in New Mexico, rich with wisdom and challenge. The centre's website, cac.org, gives information on its work and publications, and provides a daily meditation by Richard Rohr and colleagues which is appreciated by many people worldwide who aim to live with hope and love in the complex politics and crises of our time, grounded in what Rohr has called 'radical grace'.

Tom Gordon, *New Journeys Now Begin: Learning on the Path of Grief and Loss*, Wild Goose Publications, 2006.
For those of us who care about it, the destruction of life on the Earth is a grief. Writing from many years' experience of helping people through grief the author gives us many valuable insights.

Thanks

My thanks to the many people who have helped me think about these issues over the years, particularly in discussions on Iona and in my Iona Community Family Group, as well as in the Eco and the Faith & Spirituality Common Concern Networks; to members of church discussion groups, and especially those who took part in our local Lent course in 2021 when this book was beginning to take shape and we explored together some of the themes; to members of Green Christian and various smaller 'green groups' that I have been involved with; and to church members in the Diocese of Bath and Wells with whom I shared in developing an environment policy with the question of hope never far below the surface of our discussions.

Numerous writers of books and articles have also contributed, as well as television and Internet journalists; as have people in general conversations when the subject has turned to the state of the world. Sometimes simple throwaway remarks have stuck in my mind as challenges or suggestions. Three in particular have been significant and I want to thank John Davies, Tim Gorringe and the late John Williams for comments which they would soon have forgotten about but which stimulated my thinking.

In shaping my thoughts into a book it has been very helpful to know that Wild Goose Publications would take it on and I thank Sandra Kramer and Neil Paynter for that encouragement and for their detailed work.

My thanks go to everyone who read a draft of the book and gave me helpful criticism, suggestions and encouragement. You came at the subject from different angles and brought to it your very different experience and expertise. Thank you to Anne Sear, Christopher Southgate, David Ireson, Elisabeth Isted, Jo Morling, Katharine Preston, Katherine Vaughan, Peter Sear, Ran Nisbett, Richard Needle, Stephen Rymer, and Steven Palmer. I take full responsibility for what I have finally written, and am aware that on some matters we disagree. Our differences of opinion have made your critiques particularly helpful and stimulating.

Thanks too to my family who bear with me when I am distracted by mulling things over, or in a gloomy patch where thoughts about the future produce dark shadows. My youngest granddaughters, Imogen and Ayla, are a great source of joy, fun, and creativity. They also give my thoughts and fears an edge as questions about what kind of world we are leaving for our grandchildren are not simply rhetorical but very real.

Finally, my thanks, as ever, to Madron who shares my concern for the state of the world, and my exploratory faith, but leaves me to get on with my writing, even though it means me spending hours at my desk when I am supposed to be retired. Thank you for giving me the space, and for all your support.

Sources and acknowledgements

Notes

Where a very similar passage appears in two or three of the gospels I have generally given just one reference. The others can easily be found using a search engine, a website such as Bible Gateway, or a concordance.

The information on books is hopefully sufficient for them to be easily found by a bookseller or online.

Chapter 1: Optimism, hope and reason

1 It was once assumed that while people's outlook or mood could be altered by circumstances their general disposition was fixed. However, this has now been shown not to be the case. Mindfulness meditation, for example, has been proven to have an effect on the functioning of the brain so that people are happier and more resilient to stress and difficult circumstances. See Mark Williams and Danny Penman, *Mindfulness: A Practical Guide to Finding Peace in a Frantic World*, Piatkus, 2011.

2 Ed McCurdy, 'Strangest Dream'. Yes, it was 'men'. It was the sixties and that is how songs went in those days.

3 The diversion could take us back through two millennia of Western philosophy to the differences between Plato and Aristotle. There have, of course, been many views of the nature of reality in Western philosophy but the difference between Idealism and Realism runs deep. The Idealist sees the world as a manifestation of ideals or forms which exist in some other realm, with each particular object or action being a variation of the true form. The Realist sees particular objects and activities as what fundamentally exists and sees all general forms as abstractions or generalisations from the particulars. It is confused by the fact that Idealists, following Plato, think of the ideals as being real, and by the way that people are now sometimes called 'idealists' simply because they believe the world should be better than it is. They are usually called this by other people who consider themselves 'realists', but who are probably actually cynics. For further exploration into this area consult any dictionary or history of Western philosophy.

4 Interestingly, neither *The Oxford Companion to Philosophy* nor *The New Fontana Dictionary of Modern Thought* have entries on 'hope'. And neither Jürgen Moltmann's *Theology of Hope*, Tom Wright's *Surprised by Hope*, nor Richard Bauckham's and Trevor Hart's *Hope Against Hope* start with either a definition or a phenomenology of hope. It is as if they too reckon we know enough about what we mean to be able to make a start on the exploration. It is, of course, possible to have such a clear idea of what you are looking for that you cannot actually find it; like trying to buy someone the perfect Christmas present which you can imagine but which does not

actually exist, or like trying to find the ideal job. So maybe it is helpful not to be too clear.

Chapter 2: One, weird and wonderful: The world we are part of

1 The Royal Society for the Protection of Birds: one of the UK's largest conservation organisations.
2 Lovelock accepted the suggestion of his friend William Golding that he should refer not to 'interlocking feedback systems' but use the name of a Greek goddess, Gaia, as it was more likely to catch on. The idea was popularised in James Lovelock, *Gaia: A New Look at Life on Earth*, Oxford University Press, 1979, and then in many subsequent works. The name certainly caught on.
3 This possible effect of higher carbon dioxide levels in the atmosphere was first suggested in 1824. During the nineteenth century the idea was refined, including an understanding of the more powerful effect of other carbon-based gases such as methane, and laboratory tests enabled calculations and predictions to be made. It was first dubbed 'The Greenhouse Effect' in 1901.
4 For example, Saudi Arabia is currently burning 700,000 barrels of oil a day, primarily to run the country's air-conditioning systems. Peter Frankopan, *The Earth Transformed*, Bloomsbury, 2023, p. 619.
5 There have been many critiques by economists of this prioritising of growth, which are summarised by Kate Raworth in *Doughnut Economics: Seven Ways to Think Like a 21st-Century Economist*, Penguin, 2017. Raworth puts forward an alternative model for economic thinking which considers both the human and ecological impact of human activity.
6 It is not known whether Isaac Newton was really inspired to think about gravity by seeing an apple fall from a tree but it makes a good story.
7 For further elucidation and exploration on this try Carlo Rovelli, *The Order of Time*, Penguin, 2018.
8 There are numerous books for non-specialists on the current understanding of the world at both the macro and micro scales. Roger Penrose, Ian Stewart, Paul Davies, and Stephen Hawking write as scientists. John Polkinghorne, Arthur Peacocke, and Russell Stannard write as scientists and theologians. Bill Bryson wrote *A Short History of Nearly Everything*, Doubleday, 2003, for entertainment and claims to have known nothing about it before he began his research. For those in the same situation, he provides an excellent place to begin.
9 See Ian Stewart, *Does God Play Dice? The New Mathematics of Chaos*, Penguin, 1989.
10 A paper by mathematician and meteorologist Edward Norton Lorenz.
11 See Ian Stewart, *Nature's Numbers: Discovering Order and Pattern in the Universe*, Weidenfeld & Nicolson, 1995, or, John Polkinghorne, *Science and Creation: The Search for Understanding*, SPCK, 1987.

Chapter 3: Trying to make sense of people: Ten perspectives

1 See Wikipedia, *Psychopathy.*
2 Reinhold Niebuhr, *The Nature and Destiny of Man: A Christian Interpretation*, 1943
3 See, for example: Kate Raworth, *Doughnut Economics: Seven Ways to Think Like a 21st-Century Economist*, Penguin, 2017; Naomi Klein, *This Changes Everything: Capitalism versus the Climate*, Penguin, 2014; Brian McLaren, *Life After Doom: Wisdom and Courage for a World Falling Apart*, Hodder & Stoughton, 2024; Michael S. Northcott, *A Moral Climate: The Ethics of Global Warming*, Darton, Longman & Todd, 2007.
4 Over three million people died in 1932–3 during the Holodomor, a famine caused by the imposition of agricultural collectivisation by the Moscow-based regime of Stalin. This remains a significant part of the Ukrainian collective memory. For more examples of ideologically driven programmes which have been ecological and humanitarian disasters, see Peter Frankopan, *The Earth Transformed: An Untold Story*, Bloomsbury, 2023, especially the final chapters.
5 See, for example, *Paulo Freire, Cultural Action for Freedom*, Penguin, 1970, and *Pedagogy of the Oppressed*, Penguin, 1972.
6 Reinhold Niebuhr, *Moral Man and Immoral Society: A Study of Ethics and Politics*, 1932.
7 Walter Wink's *The Powers that Be: Theology for a New Millennium*, Doubleday, 1998, is a synopsis of and introduction to his earlier trilogy: *Naming the Powers: The Language of Power in the New Testament*, Fortress, 1984; *Unmasking the Powers: The Invisible Forces that Determine Human Existence*, Fortress, 1986, and *Engaging the Powers : Discernment and Resistance in a World of Domination*, Fortress, 1992.
8 For examples see: Hannah Ritchie, *Not the End of the World: Surprising Facts, Dangerous Myths and Hopeful Solutions for Our Future on Planet Earth*, Penguin, 2024.
9 For an introduction to the concept see Daniel Goleman, *Emotional Intelligence: Why It Can Matter More Than IQ*, Bloomsbury, 1996. Many personality models such as the Myers-Briggs Type Indicator and the Enneagram emphasise how emotion is significant but its influence differs between people.
10 See Wikipedia, Kama muta.
11 It has been pointed out, for example by Katrine Marçal, that while Adam Smith wrote his economic treatise *The Wealth of Nations*, in which he famously argued that people make decisions rationally for their own advantage, he was supported by his mother who did his housekeeping for no financial reward. See Katrine Marçal and Saskia Vogel, *Who Cooked Adam Smith's Dinner?: A Story about Women and Economics*, Granta, 2016. The

British government's 'austerity' programme in the 2010s, which enabled wealthy people to retain or increase their wealth, would have caused even more suffering among poorer members of society without the voluntary contributions and work of thousands of people providing and working in food banks.

Chapter 4: How we know: Information, knowledge and wisdom

1 Classic examples of paradigm shifts are the change from seeing the Earth as central to the universe to seeing it as a planet orbiting the sun; changing from seeing malaria as caused by bad air to realising it was caused by a parasite carried by mosquitos; and coming to see a garden as an ecosystem rather than a collection of plants in a plot of ground. For more on such significant changes in perception see Ian G. Barbour, *Myths, Models and Paradigms: The Nature of Scientific and Religious Language*, SCM, 1974, or, Thomas S. Kuhn, *The Structure of Scientific Revolutions*, 4th Edition, University of Chicago Press, 2012.

2 Karl Popper, 1902–1994, put forward the idea in *The Logic of Scientific Discovery*, in 1934, and it developed greater traction as the century went on. There is an obvious tension between the Popperian view of how science advances and Thomas Kuhn's concept of understanding through paradigms; a tension which generates debate and argument. But this disagreement does not stop scientists working and achieving great things, perhaps in the same way that disagreements in linguistics do not stop people speaking and writing.

3 'Economics can never be a science in the sense that physics or chemistry is. There are many different types of economic theory, each emphasising different aspects of complex reality, making different moral and political value judgements and drawing different conclusions. Moreover, economic theories fail to predict real-world developments even in areas on which they focus, not least because human beings have their own free will, unlike chemical molecules or physical objects.' Ha-Joon Chang, *Economics: The User's Guide*, Penguin, 2014, p. 5.

4 J.K. Galbraith (1908–2006) is reputed to have said, 'The only function of economic forecasting is to make astrology look respectable.' While it may actually have been said by fellow economist Ezra Solomon (1920–2002), it was characteristic of Galbraith's scepticism about the powers of economic forecasting. However, neither reckoned that economics was a waste of time. In fact, Galbraith reckoned that some understanding of economics was essential because it was the 'study of mankind in the ordinary business of life,' and without it people are manipulated by those with a better use of the economic language in order to further their own interests. John Kenneth Galbraith and Nicole Salinger *Almost Everyone's Guide to Economics*, Penguin, 1981, p. 15.

5 For more on the ways we individuals, and scientists in particular, make sense of the world see John Searle, *Mind, Language and Society: Philosophy in the Real World*, Weidenfeld & Nicolson, 1999; James W. Fowler, *Stages of Faith: The Psychology of Human Development and the Quest for Meaning*, Harper & Row, 1981.

6 In recent history this tactic has been used successfully by Adolf Hitler, Josef Stalin, Vladimir Putin and Donald Trump.

7 The English words 'practice' and 'theory' are obviously related to the Greek terms but do not mean quite the same thing. *Praxis* includes an element of reflection whereas in English 'practice' is contrasted with reflection. The English word 'theory' carries a suggestion of discontinuity with reality, whereas *theoria* was seen as the process for discovering or uncovering reality.

Chapter 5: A sense of something more: The phenomenon of religious experience

1 Despite this, many of the practitioners of religious studies have themselves been committed religious people. Of the big names in twentieth-century British religious studies Geoffrey Parrinder was a Methodist Minister, R.C. Zaehner a Roman Catholic, and Ninian Smart collaborated in writing a Christian Systematic Theology.

2 There is, for example, no Hebrew word that translates the English word 'religion'; there is only 'life'. And the term 'Hinduism' basically denotes the religion of India, which is very diverse. For criticisms of the concept see W.C. Smith, *The Meaning and End of Religion*, 1978; T. Fitzgerald, *The Ideology of Religious Studies*, 2000; or, Perry Schmidt-Leukel, 'Fractals and the World Religions Paradigm', *Modern Believing*, 65.4, Autumn 2024.

3 The term 'fundamentalist' was coined in the 1870s but became significant in 1919 when some conservative evangelicals in the USA made a declaration of what they believed were the 'fundamentals' of Christian belief. These included the idea that every word of the Bible was 'inspired by God', and that Jesus' death on the cross was a substitution for the death that was due to every human being as a result of their sin. They thought this is what 'proper' Christians had always believed, and ought to believe now. Although this is what millions of Christians in various parts of the world still believe, there are many millions of others who seriously disagree with 'the fundamentals'.

The term 'fundamentalist' has also now come to be used for Muslim groups such as the Taliban or for Hindu extremists. And whilst these groups might hate each other or, at least, see each other as unbelievers, they have in common that they hold a fixed view of how their religion should be practised and of how people should behave. Amongst fundamentalist Christians there is not only a hatred of abortion clinics and gays, and a strong conviction that everyone who is not a Christian like them will go to Hell when they die, there is also an uneasy relationship with the whole scientific view of the world. For some Christian fundamentalists evolution is simply wrong, Noah's Ark is still somewhere on Mount Ararat, and one day Jesus will come again on the clouds.

4 William James, *The Varieties of Religious Experience*, 1902, began life as the University of Edinburgh Gifford Lectures. It is still in print. Ninian Smart's similarly titled *The Religious Experience of Mankind,* 1969, is about how the phenomenon of organised religion is experienced by people, rather than about the experiences behind it.

5 Rudolph Otto, *Das Heilige*, 1917; English translation, *The Idea of the Holy*, 1923.

6 See, for example, Mary Douglas, *Natural Symbols: Explorations in Cosmology*, Routledge, 1970, on the influence of groups on interpretation, and Victor Turner, *The Ritual Process: Structure and Anti-Structure*, Aldine Transaction, 1969, on the significance of liminality, or being on the edge of a group, and of rites of passage.

7 David Hay, *Exploring Inner Space: Scientists and Religious Experience*, Mowbray, 1987, and subsequently, *Religious Experience Today: Studying the Facts*, Mowbray, 1990.

8 Peter L. Berger, *A Rumour of Angels: Modern Society and the Rediscovery of the Supernatural*, UK edition, Penguin, 1970. Although Berger used the term 'supernatural' he was not concerned with ghosts, spirits and zombies but with everyday experiences.

9 A recommended practice for people taking up mindfulness meditation is to regularly think through and count off ten good things that have happened in the last day or so, and to be grateful for them. See Mark Williams and Danny Penman, *Mindfulness: A Practical Guide to Finding Peace in a Frantic World*, Piatkus, 2011, p. 109. A century ago in evangelical Christianity this was taught as 'counting your blessings'.

10 Martin Buber, *Ich und Du*, 1923; English translations, *I and Thou*, 1937 and 1970.

11 This cultural shift from formal religion to being 'spiritual' has been studied by sociologist Grace Davie among others. See Grace Davie, *Religion in Britain since 1945: Believing without Belonging*, Blackwell, 1994; *Religion in Modern Europe: A Memory Mutates*, Oxford University Press, 2000; *Europe: The Exceptional Case*, Darton, Longman & Todd, 2002.

12 For a deeper consideration of reductionism and its inadequacy in the light of modern biology see Ian Barbour, *Nature, Human Nature and God*, SPCK, 2002.

13 See, for example, Daniel Levitin, *This is Your Brain On Music: Understanding a Human Obsession*, Atlantic, 2006; or Oliver Sacks, *Musicophilia: Tales of Music and the Brain*, Vintage Books, 2008.

14 For further exploration of the interconnection of these issues see John Searle, *Mind, Language and Society: Philosophy in the Real World*, Weidenfeld & Nicolson, 1999.

15 Such movements are often referred to as kinds of 'Idealism'. See Chapter 1, note 4.
16 For those who like such terms, this could be called 'Dual Aspect Monism'. William Blake held such a view. His challenge to Georgian and Regency English society came not only from his lifestyle and the way that his Christianity did not fit with that of the Church of England, but from the fact that to him the products of his imagination were as real as those of his senses. See John Higgs, *William Blake vs The World*, Weidenfeld & Nicolson, 2021.
17 A view which could be justly described as holistic.
18 Hence the title of Richard Dawkins' 2013 autobiography, *An Appetite for Wonder: The Making of a Scientist*.

Chapter 6: Forms of ancient wisdom: Myths, poems, and parables

1 Walter Brueggemann, *Theology of the Old Testament: Testimony, Dispute, Advocacy*, Fortress, 1997.
2 Published as James D.G. Dunn, *Unity and Diversity in the New Testament: An Inquiry into the Character of Earliest Christianity*, SCM, 1990.
3 Job 28.12; Proverbs 1.1–2.
4 G.M. Trevelyan, *English Social History*, 1942.
5 This proposal for the British fiscal system has been dubbed a 'Robin Hood Tax'.
6 For more on the nature of myth see Ian G. Barbour, *Myths, Models and Paradigms: The Nature of Scientific and Religious Language*, SCM, 1974, Chapter 2; Roy Willis, ed., *World Mythology: The Illustrated Guide*, Simon and Schuster, 1973, Introduction; or for more depth, G.S. Kirk, *Myth: Its Meaning and Functions in Ancient and Other Cultures*, Cambridge University Press, 1970; Henri Frankfort, et al., *Before Philosophy: The Intellectual Adventure of Ancient Man*, Pelican, 1949; or refer to the work of Joseph Campbell.
7 See J.R.R. Tolkien, *Tree and Leaf*, Unwin, 1964; for examples of Terry Pratchett's comic fantasies dealing with significant issues see *Equal Rites*, *Small Gods*, and *Jingo*.
8 I am grateful to The Orchard at Galhampton for this gem.
9 C.H. Dodd, *The Parables of the Kingdom*, 1935, and Joachim Jeremias, *The Parables of Jesus*, SCM, Revised edition, 1972, thought parables had one point but I disagree.
10 See Matthew 13.31–33. Luke 15.11–32 has traditionally been called 'The Prodigal Son', but is it actually about the younger son or the father who welcomes him home, or about the older brother who will not do so? Or is it about all of them? Similarly, Matthew 13.4–9 has been traditionally taken as about different people's responses to the word of God, as in the interpretative allegory that follows in verses 18–22, but is it actually about the extravagant, or prodigal, sower who spreads his seed everywhere, even on

land that will not support the plants?
11 2 Samuel 12.1–15; Jonah.

Chapter 7: Creation: Genesis, Psalms, Isaiah

1 Lamentations 1.1
2 Psalm 137.4
3 Lamentations 5.2,3
4 Genesis 1.1–2
5 The idea came from a story told by Simon Barrington-Ward at St John's College, Nottingham in 1972.
6 Is 40.28–41
7 For a more extensive development of this point see H. Richard Niebuhr, *Radical Monotheism and Western Culture*, Faber, 1961. Niebuhr argues that modern Western society is polytheistic.
8 Set to Joseph Haydn's music, it continues to be an extremely popular choral work, and was famously quoted by astronauts on first seeing the Earth from space.
9 For a more extensive exploration of the differences in approach, and the consequences of confusing them, see Karen Armstrong, *The Case for God: What Religion Really Means*, The Bodley Head, 2009.
10 See Psalm 104.16–18; Psalm 65.12–13. In the book of Job the protagonist suffers badly and argues with his friends about the reason for this. Eventually, in chapters 38–41, God answers Job directly, 'out of the whirlwind', and draws his attention to the wonder and mystery of creation.
11 Psalm 104.29–30; Genesis 1.2.
12 We have remnants of that in our speech when we talk about putting our back into something, having a handy piece of equipment, or using strong-arm tactics.
13 Ezekiel 37.1–14.
14 Isaiah 61.1 and Luke 4.18.
15 For hundreds of years people would write or speak in English about God 'himself', even though in the scriptures God was clearly neither masculine nor feminine. While the Hebrew and Greek words translated 'God' were masculine the Hebrew word translated 'spirit' or 'breath' is feminine, and very occasionally feminine images of God are used in the Hebrew texts (e.g. Isaiah 49.15) and by Jesus in the gospels (e.g. Luke 13.34, 15.8–10). More recently some people have come to write about God 'herself' and after centuries of heavy patriarchy that provides a refreshing alternative. However, the issue remains that in Hebrew and Christian thinking God is not gender-specific, but neither is God a thing, so 'it' seems inappropriate. Some writers alternate between the feminine and masculine, but I find that confusing. And the gender-neutral 'they', which is now the normal inclusive form, is also

problematic as it might suggest that God is plural. I prefer to avoid the pronouns 'he', 'she' or 'it' and refer to 'Godself' when necessary, even though some readers might find it clunky or strange. For an extensive discussion of the use of gender-specific language about God see Elizabeth A. Johnson, *She Who Is: The Mystery of God in Feminist Theological Discourse*, Crossroad, 2002.

16 See, for example, Amos 5 or Isaiah 40.

17 e.g. Ezekiel 31.

18 e.g. Jeremiah 24; Amos 7.

19 e.g. Ezekiel 37.

Chapter 8: God and humanity: Genesis, Psalms, Amos, Micah

1 Joshua 6; Judges 6.36–40; Exodus 3.1–4.17

2 1 Kings 21

3 Nimrod appears briefly in Genesis 10.8, and Magog in Genesis 10.2. He also appears as a place in Ezekiel 38.1, and as a ghostly warrior in Revelation 20.8. Elgar, of course, dedicated one of his Enigma variations to a friend who was nicknamed Nimrod. Perhaps, somewhere, there is another piece of music dedicated to Magog.

4 Genesis 2.7

5 Genesis 2.15f

6 See Claus Westermann, *Creation,* English translation, SPCK, 1974, p. 93f

7 Genesis 4

8 Genesis 6–9

9 Genesis 11.1–10

10 Because the story is a poorly edited conflation of two old tales it has both. Compare Genesis 7.2 with 7.15.

11 One of Augustine's contemporary critics was Pelagius. Pelagius lost the intellectual battle among the Mediterranean churches. Augustine was a Latin scholar and orator whereas Pelagius was a Celtic monk, and he was criticised not only for his views but for teaching women and eating porridge. His name became a byword for heresy but for a reassessment of Pelagius see M. Forthomme Nicholson, 'Celtic Theology: Pelagius', in James P. Mackey, ed., *An Introduction to Celtic Christianity*, T&T Clark, 1989. See also James P. Mackey, *Christianity and Creation: A Systematic Theology*, Continuum, 2006, pp. 88–95; and Alister E. McGrath, *Christian Theology: An Introduction*, Second Edition, Blackwell, 1997, pp. 426–432.

12 Genesis 9.20–23; Genesis 12.10–20; 2 Samuel 11.1–12.23; 1 Kings 2.10–11.41; 1 Kings 19.1–18; 2 Kings 2.23–24.

Chapter 9: God's freedom: Exodus, Proverbs, Amos, Micah

1 It is confusing, not least because some of the people in the stories have several names, which is possibly because some stories about different people were

amalgamated to being about one person. In the saga which takes up Genesis 12–36, nomadic Abraham, who was also called Abram, had a son called Ishmael, by a servant called Hagar, and another son called Isaac, by his wife Sarai or Sarah. Isaac inherited the patriarchal role and had twin sons by his wife Rebekah. The first born was called Esau, or Edom, and should have become head of the family but the second son, Jacob, tricked him out of his inheritance. Jacob instead became the patriarch, and was also called Israel. Jacob then had twelve sons, one of whom was Judah from whom the Jews derived their name, and another was Joseph, of dreamcoat fame. Behind these stories, which were passed on for generations, lie competition, jealousy and feuding between various tribes of Ishmaelites, Edomites, and Israelites, together with a recognition that they were more closely related to each other than they were to some other people, like the Hittites, Ammonites and Egyptians.

2 This story is in Exodus 1–4.

3 The word 'righteous' is rarely used today outside a traditional Christian religious context. The word 'self-righteous' is probably more common, and is an undesirable character trait, whereas to be 'righteous' was highly desirable. The word integrity captures something of the meaning of righteousness in some contexts.

4 Exodus 3.14.

5 For more on the nature and significance of the name see Gerhard von Rad, *Old Testament Theology*, Volume 1, SCM, 1975, pp. 179–187; Walter Eichrodt, *Theology of the Old Testament*, Volume 1, SCM, 1961, pp. 187–192.

6 This summary was quoted by Jesus in Mark 12.29–31.

7 i.e. A man wanted to know that the son who would inherit his property was actually his son, so adultery was forbidden. A wife was also seen as the property of the man so a man having sex with another man's wife was seen as a theft from the other man. Jesus' angle on this was interesting and radically different. In his interpretation a man could commit the offence of adultery against his ex-wife by marrying another woman. The relationship was therefore mutual, not one of possession. See Mark 10.1–12, etc.

8 See Deuteronomy 30.19–20.

9 See Hosea 11.1–4.

10 See Ezekiel 20.40–44.

11 Isaiah 35 is a beautiful poem of celebration and hopefulness.

12 Amos 1.

13 Isaiah 41.25; 45.1f.

14 Genesis 12.3.

15 Exodus 19.6.

16 Psalm 24.1.

17 See also Isaiah 2.1–4.

18 Ecclesiastes 3.1–11; 11.7–10; 12.12.

Chapter 10: Jesus and the reign of God: Matthew, Mark, Luke

1 The scepticism was not based on a lack of historical evidence, although there was not as much evidence as people often assumed, but derived largely from a philosophical position which claimed that faith should not be based on historical or scientific evidence. This view, articulated by the eighteenth-century writer G.E. Lessing, was that 'the accidental truths of history can never become the proof of necessary truths of reason', and it became an accepted view within German Liberal Protestantism. It then morphed, under the influence of existentialism, into a view that a reasonable theology should not only not be based on historical evidence but should have no historical connection at all. This view began to fade in the nineteen sixties when theologians and historians who had grown up with this view began a 'new quest for the historical Jesus' and found that there was actually quite a lot of evidence.

2 *The Greatest Story Ever Told* was the title of a 1965 Hollywood movie for which the storyline was an amalgam of episodes from all four gospels. It begins with the Magi visiting the child Jesus (from Matthew), has Thomas questioning the appearance of the risen Jesus to his disciples (from John) and ends with Jesus ascending into Heaven (from Luke), but in the film Jesus' Ascension is accompanied by the 'Hallelujah Chorus' (words from Revelation with music by Handel).

3 Anyone familiar with the gospels can quickly think of passages which stretch their imagination, such as angels singing in the sky, a star leading magi from the East, Jesus walking on water, or Jesus feeding five thousand people. Nasty bits are often glossed over but in Mark 7.24–30 Jesus insults a Syrophoenician woman, in Matthew 21.19 he curses a fig tree, and in Matthew 27.25 the crowd tells Pilate that the responsibility for Jesus' death should rest on them and their children, a passage which gave rise to the medieval and later accusation that Jews were 'Christ-killers'.

4 Geza Vermes, *Jesus in His Jewish Context, SCM,* 2003, p. 52.

5 Matthew 5.17–20.

6 Only these four were included within the canon of the New Testament but other 'gospels' were written within a couple of centuries of Jesus, and fragments of some of these remain. Most are reckoned to be later than the canonical four, although 'The Gospel of Thomas' is possibly not and contains interesting unique material. There is a view known as the Synoptic Hypothesis which has been around for nearly two centuries. This is that Mark's gospel was the first gospel to be written and that the writers of Matthew and Luke used it and added material from other sources to compile their gospels. While it has wide acceptance, not everyone agrees. There are those who think that the gospels must be historically accurate because they are inspired by God, despite all the irreconcilable differences, and

others who think that Matthew's must have been written first because one of the Church Fathers said so. Among those who do not cling to these views there are New Testament scholars who argue that Luke used Matthew, a view known as the Farrer Hypothesis after its originator, the British scholar Austin Farrer. And there are other views around.

7 For an introduction to the portraits of Jesus in the four gospels try Richard A. Burridge, *Four Gospels, One Jesus? A Symbolic Reading*, SPCK, 1994, with several subsequent editions, USA publication by Eerdmans, and numerous translations. On the subject of the historical Jesus see E.P. Sanders, *The Historical Figure of Jesus*, Penguin, 1993; Gerd Theissen and Annette Merz, *The Historical Jesus: A Comprehensive Guide*, SCM, 1998; and for the social background to the gospels see Bruce J. Malina, *The New Testament World: Insights from Cultural Anthropology*, SCM, 1981; and Wolfgang Stegemann, Bruce J. Malina, Gerd Theissen, eds. *The Social Setting of Jesus and the Gospels*, Fortress, 2002.

8 Hosea 11.1–4.

9 See Proverbs 3.12, Psalm 68.5.

10 For example, Matthew 6.9; 6.32; 7.11; etc.

11 Luke 15.4–7 and Luke 15.8–9.

12 Luke 10.38–42. This story about two sisters, Mary and Martha, has been traditionally interpreted to suggest that a contemplative life is better than an active one, so it was better to be a monk or nun than a doctor or social activist. However, in the society of the time Mary would have been bringing shame on her family by joining the men and listening to the rabbi, but Jesus defends her from criticism by her sister.

13 Luke 8.1–3.

14 Luke 7.36–50. In Matthew 21.31 he tells the Chief Priests and Elders that the tax collectors and prostitutes are going into the reign of God before them. For a study of attitudes towards sex in the New Testament world and the pitfalls of reading back into the texts later European attitudes and values, see L. William Countryman, *Dirt, Greed and Sex: Sexual Ethics in the New Testament and Their Implications for Today*, SCM, 1989.

15 As with the Iona Community.

16 It is attributed to the *New Zealand Prayer Book*, published by the Anglican Church, although the online version has in its liturgies the version authorised by the International Convention on English Texts.

17 Luke 15.11–32.

18 Matthew 9.13; 12.7; quoting Hosea 6.6.

19 As in the popular Christmas readings: Isaiah 9.6–7; 11.1–3; Micah 5.2–4.

20 e.g. Psalm 10.16; 29.10.

21 As in Isaiah 9.7 and Micah 5.2f.

22 I Samuel 8.

23 'The new thing in the teaching of Jesus is not the combination of the

metaphors of father and king but something which is not obvious at first sight: Jesus never speaks of God as "king".' Gerd Theissen & Annette Merz, *The Historical Jesus: A Comprehensive Guide*, SCM, 1996, p. 274.

24 Jesus' basic message according to Matthew and Mark was that the reign of God was at hand, and throughout the synoptic gospels Jesus tells parables about 'the kingdom'. See, for example: Matthew 13.1–47.

25 Examples of apocalyptic literature made their way into the Hebrew scriptures in Daniel and Zechariah, but there was a lot more of it around and many people would have understood Jesus' message as heralding this great day. Mark 9.47, Mark 10.15 and 10.17 can be read that way and when Jesus uses the phrase 'on that day' it might be seen as a reference to the cataclysm.

26 Matthew 6.1–4; 7.22; 24.36; Mark 10.29–43; etc.

27 For example: Matthew 13.31–33.

28 In Luke's version of this story Jesus says 'by the finger of God', which is probably an older version. See Luke 11.14–23.

29 Matthew 11.2–6, referring to Isaiah 35.5–6.

30 Matthew 13.31–33.

31 The Greek can be translated as 'among' or 'within'.

32 Daniel 7.13.

33 Ezekiel 37.3, etc.

34 Matthew 24.37, etc. compared with Matthew 11.19, etc.

35 E.P. Sanders, *The Historical Figure of Jesus,* Penguin, 1993, p. 178. See also Gerd Theissen and Annette Merz, *The Historical Jesus: A Comprehensive Guide*, SCM, 1998, p. 240f; Joachim Jeremias, *New Testament Theology, Vol. 1*, SCM, 1971, p. 96f; Geza Vermes, *Jesus in His Jewish Context*, SCM, 2003, p. 27f.

36 Matthew 24.1–25.46 compared with Matthew 18.1–35.

37 As in Luke 2.32.

38 e.g. Albert Schweitzer, *The Quest of the Historical Jesus*, 1906.

39 e.g. Many Anglican Sunday School teachers.

40 e.g. Ched Myers, *Binding the Strong Man: A Political Reading of Mark's Story of Jesus*, Orbis, 1988.

41 e.g. C.H. Dodd, *The Founder of Christianity*, Collins, 1970.

42 e.g. Rudolph Bultmann, *Jesus and the Word*, 1934.

43 E.P. Sanders, ibid, p. 178.

Chapter 11: What happened to Jesus: Matthew, Mark, Luke, Acts

1 Hence the saying ascribed to Desmond Tutu: 'When people tell me you can't mix religion and politics, I wonder what Bible they've been reading.'

2 Matthew 5.17f and Matthew 7.18f.

3 Among others, Psalms 1, 19, and 119 praise God for the Torah.

4 See Matthew 12.14, and 23.1–36 which should be essential reading for anyone brought up on the 'Gentle Jesus, meek and mild' idea.

5 For this reason, childlessness was seen as a great curse. 1 Samuel 1 and Luke 1.5–24 are stories of women relieved of the 'shame' of childlessness by having a baby.

6 Daniel 12.2.

7 Isaiah 26.19, Ezekiel 37.

8 Job 19.25, now a well-known passage thanks to Handel's *Messiah*.

9 For example, during Jesus' childhood there was a rebellion against Rome known as the Robber War and Galilee was one centre of revolt. 'Judas the Galilean' was a rebel who taught that taxes should not be paid to the Romans, and two of his sons, Simon and Jacob, were later crucified for insurrection. For more information see Gerd Theissen and Annette Merz, *The Historical Jesus*, SCM, 1998, pps. 162–180; and Wolfgang Stegemann, Bruce J. Malina and Gerd Theissen, eds. *The Social Setting of Jesus and the Gospels*, Fortress Press, 2002, especially pps. 223–332.

10 Sadducees took their name from Zadok, a priest at the time of David and Solomon, who has been made even more famous by G.F. Handel whose *Zadok the Priest* has been sung at the coronations of British monarchs since 1727; which says something about the pretensions of British monarchists. In 1992 it was used as the anthem for the UEFA Champions League although the connection of Zadok with football remains obscure.

11 The story is told in all four gospels. In Matthew 21, Mark 11, and Luke 19 it is as Jesus comes to Jerusalem for the last time having toured and taught in Galilee for perhaps several years. In John 2 it is before Jesus' work in Galilee.

12 Matthew 22.15–33 and Luke 20.20–38.

13 As told in the books of Maccabees, which were not later included in the canon of the Hebrew Scriptures but are in the Roman Catholic Bible and the Protestant Apocrypha.

14 A significant source of information about the time of Jesus comes from the Jewish historian Josephus and, according to him, the term 'Zealot' arose during the Jewish War which led to the destruction of Jerusalem in 70 CE. However, Luke 6.15 mentions a disciple called Simon the Zealot. It is possible the term was in use before the war, but only then came to be used widely.

15 Matthew 5.43–48; Matthew 5.38–42. For a detailed argument on why this second passage should be considered as advocating creative non-violence see Walter Wink, *Engaging the Powers: Discernment and Resistance in a World of Domination*, Augsburg Fortress, 1992. For a summary see David Osborne, *The Owl and the Stereo: An Introduction to Radical Christianity*, Wild Goose Publications, 1997.

16 Luke 6.32–36.

17 Zechariah 9.9.

18 Deuteronomy 21.23 quoted in Galatians 3.13.

19 Mark 15.34; Matthew 27.46 and Psalm 22.1.

20 Luke 23.39–43.

21 Mark 15.42–46, and also the other three gospels. Joseph of Arimathea, who is said to have given the tomb, is a mysterious character who appears at this point in all four gospels but nowhere else. This combination of a significant role in the narrative combined with a lack of other information gave great scope for legends developing down the centuries. In one such tale he was Jesus' uncle and a tin trader who came to Britain and brought the young Jesus with him to Glastonbury, and then later brought the cup from the Last Supper, the Holy Grail. There is absolutely no evidence for any of this but that does not stop English storytellers and Glastonbury traders from continuing to peddle the idea.

22 See Matthew 28, Mark 16, Luke 24 and John 21–22.

23 What David Jenkins, Bishop of Durham, actually said was, 'I am not clear that God manoeuvres physical things … After all, a conjuring trick with bones only proves that it is as clever as a conjuring trick with bones … A resuscitated corpse might be a resuscitated corpse and might be the sign of something, but there is still the question of what it is the symbol of.' *Of the Resurrection*, in 'Poles Apart', BBC Radio, 4th October, 1984.

24 Among others it is the view of Ched Myers, *Binding the Strong Man*, Orbis, 1988; and C.M.Tuckett, who writes in *The Oxford Bible Commentary*, 2001, 'The rest of the gospel is to be completed by the reader. But the reader can only complete the story by following as a disciple of Mark's Jesus … Being prepared to follow in the way of discipleship as spelt out by him, i.e. the way of the cross. There, and only there, will Jesus be "seen" and experienced.' p. 922. There are other interpretations of the abrupt ending, including the rather more prosaic ones that for some reason Mark simply never finished the book, or that his ending got lost.

25 Matthew 28.19–20.

26 Whether 'sky' is a living or a dead metaphor for the realm of God depends perhaps on the context but, given the glorious possibilities, even this is understated. Jesus does not have a fiery chariot like the prophet Elijah in 2 Kings 2.11. And there are no heavenly hosts to greet him: that is left for medieval artists and Hollywood to conjure up.

27 Luke 24.51; Acts 2.

28 Luke 24.13–35.

29 For example, Isaiah 53.

30 Compare Luke 9.12–17; Luke 22.14–20; Acts 2.42; 1 Corinthians 11.23–25.

Chapter 12: Talking about God: Problems and possibilities

1 In his Gifford Lectures Michael Polanyi argued that in any scientific investigation the researcher will have an initial position, a perspective on the subject, and be emotionally involved in their enquiry. That is not a problem.

Problems arise for a scientist, or any other thinker, when they do not recognise their involvement in the subject. See Michael Polanyi, *Personal Knowledge: Towards a Post-Critical Philosophy*, 1958.

2 *Texts of Terror* is the title of a 2003 book by feminist biblical scholar Phyllis Trible in which she looks closely at four stories in which women are severely abused. Her work with these Bible texts has application to many other passages, and relevance to anyone who values the Bible and is concerned for human respect and social justice.

3 As in the books of Joshua and Judges.

4 Luke 8.1–3; Luke 7.1–10; Matthew 5.38–42.

5 Many of us make up stories, do puzzles, get engrossed in novels, work at pure mathematics or engage in analytical philosophy, and we all dream. These are all healthy and often useful activities. Problems can arise if we are not aware of the boundary between imagination and physical reality. Exploring that boundary could take us into many fascinating areas, such as the nature of mental health, postmodern philosophy, speculation as to how stable or functional a 'post-truth' society can be, or whether Donald Trump really believed he won the 2020 Presidential election. But we are focussed on the theme of hope.

6 Epistemologists will probably identify this as a form of Critical Realism. It is a way of seeing the world which is held by many scientists and not a few theologians, including, for example: Wolfhart Pannenberg, Jürgen Moltmann, Keith Ward, John Hick, Tom Wright, James Dunn, and Thomas Torrance; and scientist theologians such as Ian Barbour, Arthur Peacocke and John Polkinghorne. While it is by no means the only approach in our Western culture, critical realists will probably see theirs as common sense, although there is always doubt as to whether 'common sense' really exists. For an exploration of theological realism, non-realism and anti-realism, see Marcus J. Borg, *The Heart of Christianity*, Harper, 2003, especially pps. 61–79; Colin Crowder, ed., *God and Reality*, Mowbray, 1997; John Hick, *The Fifth Dimension: An Exploration of the Spiritual Realm*, Oneworld, 1999; and Hans Küng, *On Being a Christian*, Collins, 1978, pps. 57–88.

Chapter 13: Creation now: Cosmic art

1 This has arrogantly and unfortunately been dubbed 'The Anthropic Principle' because without this fine tuning we humans would not exist. But neither would mosquitos.

2 See, for example, on the one hand, Martin Rees, *Just Six Numbers*, Weidenfeld & Nicolson, 1999, who argues ultimately for coincidence, and on the other, John Polkinghorne, *One World*, SPCK, 1987, who believes there is a creator.

3 As an answer to the age-old question of why the world exists, the cosmological argument is very limited. To put it bluntly, if we say, 'God made (or

makes) the cosmos', the next question is obviously, 'Who or what made (or makes) God?' But, as a minimum, seeing the cosmos as created can be understood as a statement about the nature and value of the cosmos. To explore this issue in further depth see, for example: John Hick, *Philosophy of Religion*, 4th Edition, Pearson, 1989; John MacQuarrie, *Principles of Christian Theology*, Revised Edition, SCM, 1977; Hans Kung, *Does God Exist?*, Collins, 1980; or Karen Armstrong, *The Question of God: What Religion Really Means*, The Bodley Head, 2009.

4 Mozart is reputed to have said, 'The music is not in the notes, but in the silence between.' A composer will use silence within a piece of music but, unlike notes, the players do not have to make the silence: they have to refrain from playing and give space to the silence which lies behind. This can possibly be developed as an approach to spirituality, continuing with the metaphor of silence for God.

5 Augustine of Hippo (354–430) speculated on God being beyond time in his *Confessions*. The idea was developed further by Boethius (480–524) in his *Consolation of Philosophy*, written while he was in prison awaiting execution: the kind of situation which is said to sharpen the mind considerably.

6 As songwriter Sydney Carter succinctly put it:
'You can blame it onto Adam, you can blame it onto Eve,
You can blame it on the Devil, but that I can't believe.
It was God who made the Devil and the woman and the man,
And there wouldn't be an apple if it wasn't in the plan.'
Sydney Carter (1915–2004), 'Friday Morning'

7 I have lived for over seventy years which have so far been relatively comfortable. My daughter Miriam lived for just eleven days after her birth and during that time she was sedated to reduce the pain from her broken soft bones. In the womb she had had no analgaesic.

8 This correlation is explored by Peter L. Berger in *A Rumour of Angels*, Penguin, 1969, especially chapter 3.

9 This interplay is explored by Tim Gorringe, using particularly the image of a drama, in T.J. Gorringe *God's Theatre: A Theology of Providence*, SCM, 1991. The director of a play does not determine each and every action or the way words are said. There is an interplay between the author, the director and the actors. If the actors had no freedom there could be no great actors. Some drama productions begin with a fairly blank sheet and an outline idea rather than a tightly written script. The popular American comedy *Friends* began with the director seeing how the assembled cast would interact. Jürgen Moltmann in *God in Creation*, SCM, 1985, p. 156, speaks of the space of creation existing within the space of God. Ruth Page speaks of God's 'companionship' with the world, in *God and the Web of Creation*, SCM, 1996, p. 154f. They are all employing images which, with varying degrees of success, balance the idea of the cosmos being both God's creation

and having a degree of freedom. Page speaks of God 'letting possibility be'. It is an experience many of us have as teachers, managers or parents when we balance guidance and boundaries with freedom and expression, not determining what the student, colleague or child will do but wanting to help them develop their insights and skills well.

Chapter 14: A dynamic Trinity: Creative, expressive, active

1 Compare John 1.1–18 and Genesis 1–2.
2 Matthew 28.19.
3 Sam Keen, *To a Dancing God*, Harper & Row, 1970.
4 'Father, Lord of Creation', by Stewart Cross (1928–1989).
5 See, for example, *The Courage to Be*, Nisbet, 1952, p. 176f.
6 St Patrick is reputed to have explained the concept of the Trinity by pointing to a shamrock with its three leaves on one stem. Early Irish theology was much more subtle than that so the church's thinking either developed very quickly or the story of the great missionary using this simple image is a legend with little historical basis. Probably the latter. But that does not stop the Ireland rugby team having shamrocks on their shirts while the England team have roses.
7 This way of thinking about the relationship between God and the cosmos can be described as a form of *panentheism*. The word was only coined in the early nineteenth century but this way of thinking is much older and might be seen in the New Testament, for example in Colossians 3.11, and the teaching of Jesus in the gospels. Among the many theologians of recent decades who have been panentheists are Leonardo Boff, Charles Hartshorne, Sallie McFague, John MacQuarrie, Jürgen Moltmann, and Arthur Peacocke. For further discussion see Elizabeth A. Johnson, *She Who Is*, Crossroad, 2002, pp. 230–236. For online information on panentheism in world religions look at Wikipedia, or for a detailed study of panentheism in Judaism and Christianity go to the *Stanford Encyclopedia of Philosophy*. Note that panentheism is not the same as *pantheism*, which is the belief that God is in every thing because God is the totality of everything.
8 'Prior to the seventeenth century, the word "believe" did not mean believing in the truth of statements or propositions, whether problematic or not. Grammatically, the object of believing was not statements, but a person. Moreover, the contexts in which it is used in premodern English make it clear that it meant: to hold dear; to prize; to give one's loyalty to; to give one's self to; to commit oneself. It meant … faithfulness, allegiance, loyalty, commitment, and trust. Most simply, "to believe" meant "to love". Indeed, the English words "believe" and "belove" are related. What we believe is what we belove. Faith is about beloving God … To believe in God is to belove God. Faith is about beloving God and all that God beloves … Faith

is the way of the heart.' Marcus Borg, *The Heart of Christianity*, Harper, 2003, p. 40.

9 The nearest the gospels come to this is John 11.26 and 27 where Jesus says that those who trust in him will live, even if they die, and asks Lazarus's sister Mary if she believes this. She then affirms it and goes further by declaring that she believes he is the Messiah and Son of God.

10 See Psalms 104 and 147.

Chapter 15: God and us: Love and suffering

1 Matthew 4.1, Luke 13.16, Matthew 16.23, etc.

2 Romans 6.5–11.

3 Revelation 12.7–9.

4 It seems likely that thinking of the world as a theatre of conflict between God and Satan, or the Devil, and their legions of angels came into Jewish thinking from Zoroastrianism, the dominant religion of the Persians at the time they conquered Babylon. The Persians allowed Jewish exiles to return to Palestine and were the dominant power in the region until the conquests of Alexander the Great two centuries later. Zoroastrian dualism continued to be influential and by the time of Jesus thought about Satan and demons was mainstream throughout the Eastern Mediterranean.

5 See Chapter 8.

6 See Luke 15.6–7; John 10.1–18.

7 As in Luke 1.46–55: The Magnificat.

8 See Chapter 11.

9 Christians have often spoken of Jesus taking on the sin of the World. If, as I have suggested, the debilitating and sometimes destructive features of humanity constitute what is meant by 'sin', in his trial and crucifixion Jesus is fully caught up in the matrix of sin.

10 Mark 15.34; Galatians 3.13; Deuteronomy 21.22–23.

11 Colossians 1.15; Hebrews 1.1–3; John 1.14.

12 From 'The Suffering God' in *The Unutterable Beauty,* 1927.

13 Dietrich Bonhoeffer, *Letters and Papers from Prison*, SCM, 1953.

14 Jürgen Moltmann, *The Crucified God*, SCM, 1974, p. 248.

Chapter 16: New creation: Life out of death

1 C.S. Lewis was adamant that the gospels were not legends because he had read lots of legends and the gospels were very different. They certainly are very different from the many tales of King Arthur or Robin Hood, but that does not mean that what we read in the gospels did not develop in the period between the life of Jesus and the books being written.

2 Luke 7.11–17; 8.40–56; John 11.38–44.

3 1 Cor 12.4–31.

4 John 20.19–23; Matthew 28.20; Luke 24.50 & Acts 2.1–4; Romans 8.9–11. For more on Paul's strong linking of the Spirit and Jesus see 2 Corinthians 3.17, Galatians 4.6, Philippians 1.19. For an in-depth study see James D. G. Dunn, *Jesus and the Spirit*, SCM, 1975.

5 Wolfhart Pannenberg, *Jesus God and Man*, SCM, 1968, pps. 88–106; *The Apostles' Creed*, SCM, 1972, pps. 96–115.

6 Lk 4.18.

7 Rom 14.17.

8 Colossians 1.15; John 1.14.

9 See Jürgen Moltmann, *The Crucified God*, SCM, 1974, and W.H. Vanstone, *Love's Endeavour, Love's Expense*, Darton Longman & Todd, 1977. See also Elizabeth Johnson, *She Who Is: The Mystery of God in Feminist Theological Discourse*, Crossroad, 1992, Chapter 12; John V. Taylor, *The Christlike God*, SCM, 1992, Chapter 5; James P. Mackey, *The Christian Experience of God as Trinity*, SCM, 1983, Chapter 14.

10 Matthew 26.30.

11 See John V. Taylor, *The Go-Between God: The Holy Spirit and the Christian Mission*, SCM, 1972; Jürgen Moltmann, *The Spirit of Life: A Universal Affirmation*, SCM, 1992.

12 Revelation 1.8.

13 *The Guardian,* 19th March, 2023.

14 See, for example: C.H. Dodd, *The Founder of Christianity*, Collins, 1970; Ched Myers, *Binding the Strong Man*, Orbis,1997; Wolfhart Pannenberg, *The Apostles Creed*, SCM, 1972; Kathryn Tanner, *Jesus, Humanity and the Trinity*, Fortress, 2001, and *Eschatology and Ethics*, in Gilbert Meilaender and William Werpehowski, *The Oxford Handbook of Theological Ethics*, 2005, p. 41f. For an interweaving of various threads see Rowan Williams, *Resurrection: Interpreting the Easter Gospel*, Darton, Longman & Todd, 2002.

15 Revelation 21.3–7.

16 See Chapter 6.

17 According to Acts 17.28, this phrase from the Greek poet Aratus was used by Paul when he was preaching in Athens. It accords with Job 12.10 and Daniel 5.23.

18 1 Corinthians 15.35–41; John 12.24.

19 1 Corinthians 15.42–49.

20 Whereas both the Apostles' Creed and the Nicene Creed declare belief in 'the resurrection of the body'.

21 This way of seeing resurrection is developed by Harry Williams in H.A. Williams, *True Resurrection*, Mitchell Beazley, 1972.

22 A symposium of scientists and theologians on resurrection came up with the image of information being transferred from one computer to another so that the new hardware picks up not only data but also the programmes. See John Polkinghorne, *The God of Hope and the End of the World*, SPCK, 2002.

23 Romans 8.18–25; 2 Corinthians 5.17; Revelation 21.1–5.
24 As Psalm 118.24, a Fijian worship song, and the morning prayers of the Iona Community put it: 'This is the day that the Lord has made, we will rejoice and be glad in it.'
25 Romans 8.38–39.

Chapter 17: Wisdom and hope

1 Proverbs 8.22–36.
2 1 Samuel 3.7; Hosea 1.2; Zechariah 4.6; Malachi 1.2; etc.
3 Prophets were not primarily people who foretold the future, although they could sometimes see where things were going.
4 For a more comprehensive discussion of the place of wisdom in creation and its reference in John's gospel see Celia Deane-Drummond, *Creation Through Wisdom: Theology and the New Biology*, T & T Clark, 2000; Martin Scott, *Sophia and the Johannine Jesus*, Sheffield Academic Press, 1992; Elizabeth Johnson, *She Who Is: The Mystery of God in Feminist Theological Discourse*, Crossroad Publishing, 2002.
5 Matthew 5–7.
6 Luke 15.11–32; 10.29–37.
7 Matthew 13.
8 John 4.10; 6.35; 15.1; 8.12; 10.14; 14.6.
9 Grandiosity, or narcissism perhaps, but without access to the client a psychological assessment cannot be carried out, however strong the evidence of a disorder.
10 There is a view that when you read the gospels you have to conclude that Jesus was either mad, bad or God. Or, in another version, either a liar, a lunatic or the Lord. C.S. Lewis presents this trilemma in *Mere Christianity*, although he did not invent it. However, it is based on the premise that everything the gospels relate is what Jesus of Nazareth actually said and did, which many New Testament scholars do not think is the case. See Wikipedia, Lewis' Trilemma.
11 John also says 'the Light that enlightens every person was coming into the world' (John 1.9). People with an exclusive view read that as 'the light that enlightens every Christian', or, 'the light that could enlighten every person', but that is not what it says.
12 Matthew 5.17.
13 Matthew 6.24.
14 Exodus 20.16.
15 Matthew 5.37.
16 Matthew 15.1–6.
17 Deuteronomy 5.29.
18 Matthew 18.1–14; 19.13–15; Luke 9.46–48.

19 There are numerous writers, activists and organisations specifically applying the wisdom of the Hebrew scriptures and the New Testament to the ecological crisis. See, for example: the 2015 Papal Encyclical *Laudato Si': On Care for Our Common Home*, and its accompanying study materials; Katharine Preston, *Field with a View: Science and Faith*, Wild Goose Publications, 2023; Sarah Tillett, ed. *Caring for Creation: Biblical and Theological Perspectives*, Bible Reading Fellowship, 2005; Martin J.Hodson and Margot R.Hodson, *Cherishing the Earth: How to Care for God's Creation*, Monarch Books, 2008; Catherine von Ruhland, *Living with the Planet: Making a Difference in a Time of Climate Change*, Lion, 2008; *Sharing God's Planet: A Christian Vision for a Sustainable Future*, Church House Publishing, 2005; Celia E. Deane Drummond, *The Ethics of Nature*, Blackwell, 2004. For organisations in the UK see the work of Green Christian, the Iona Community, Eco-Congregation, A Rocha and its Eco-Church programme, Christian Aid, and Operation Noah.

20 For an informed survey of the development of the church see Diarmaid MacCulloch, *A History of Christianity: The First Three Thousand Years*, Penguin, 2010. For more information on the early years see, for example, Gerd Theissen, *The First Followers of Jesus: A Sociological Analysis of the Earliest Christianity, SCM, 2012;* or for more depth: Philip F. Esler, ed. *Modelling Early Christianity: Social Scientific studies of the New Testament in its context*, Routledge, 1995; or Wayne A. Meeks, *The First Urban Christians: The Social World of the Apostle Paul*, Yale University Press, 1983.

21 John 16.13.

22 1 Corinthians 12.3; Matthew 7.24–27.

23 For a very small sample of people working in this field who have had an explicit faith consider Frank Lake (Clinical Theology, working from a largely Freudian perspective), Christopher Bryant (drawing on the work of C.G. Jung), Mark Williams (Mindfulness), M. Scott Peck (*The Road Less Travelled*), Thomas Harris (Transactional Analysis); but most Christian and Jewish therapists acknowledge an enormous debt to the insights of others without faith.

24 Mark 10.13–16. See Bruce Reed, *The Dynamics of Religion: Process and Movement in Christian Churches*, Darton, Longman & Todd, 1978. Like many writers on faith development James W. Fowler in *Stages of Faith: The Psychology of Human Development and the Quest for Meaning*, Harper and Row, 1981, sees letting go of rigid mental constructs as an important part of development and an overall movement towards a maturity which is a kind of childlikeness. See also Richard Rohr, *Simplicity: The Freedom of Letting Go*, Crossroad, 1991.

25 See for example: Gustavo Gutiérrez, *A Theology of Liberation: History, Politics and Salvation*, Orbis, 1973; Jon Sobrino, *Jesus the Liberator: A Historical-Theological Reading of Jesus of Nazareth*, Burns & Oates, 1994; Doro-

thee Sölle, *On Earth as in Heaven: A Liberation Spirituality of Sharing*, Westminster John Knox, 1993; Walter Brueggemann, *The Prophetic Imagination*, 2nd Edition, Augsburg Fortress, 2001; T.J. Gorringe, *Furthering Humanity: A Theology of Culture*, Ashgate, 2004; Kathy Galloway, *Sharing the Blessing: Overcoming Poverty and Working for Justice*, SPCK & Christian Aid, 2008; Jürgen Moltmann, *Ethics of Hope*, SCM, 2012.

26 Walter Wink, *The Powers That Be: Theology for a New Millennium*, Doubleday, 1998.

27 Mark 11.1–6 and Mark 14.12–16.

28 Matthew 10.16.

29 See Dietrich Bonhoeffer, *Ethics*, especially Part One, Sections III and VI, SCM, 1955.

30 It is important to bear in mind that for Bonhoeffer there was no democratic option: he was living in a totalitarian regime. There are people who claim to be following his teaching and advocating violence even when other options are available. Anyone who wants to claim Bonhoeffer as an inspiration should first read *The Cost of Discipleship*, SCM, 1959.

31 Clearly many people feel that the Earth is doomed as a home for humanity. Theologian Brian McLaren, *Life After Doom: Wisdom and Courage for a World Falling Apart*, Hodder & Stoughton, 2024, is sceptical about whether the present global civilisation can avoid collapse. However, data scientist Hannah Ritchie, *Not the End of the World: Surprising Facts, Dangerous Myths and Hopeful Solutions for Our Future on Planet Earth*, Penguin, 2024, reckons we are pulled into a debilitating sense of disaster by headlines rather than the big picture and that, while things are definitely bad, there is actually still the possibility of a sustainable future, although society will need to change considerably and quickly. This is also the view of Kate Raworth, *Doughnut Economics: Seven Ways to Think Like a 21st-Century Economist*, Penguin, 2017. For both of them the future of society has to be very different from the present and for those who benefit greatly from the present system that will perhaps feels like a disaster.

Chapter 18: Living hope

1 There are a great many books about different spiritual practices. As an introduction to the range of possible practices which can help us in this time of ecological crisis see David Osborne, *Love for the Future: A Journey*, Wild Goose Publications, 2013; Anne Richards, *Sense Making Faith: Body, Spirit, Journey*, CTBI, 2007; or David Runcorn, *Spirituality Workbook: A Guide for Explorers, Pilgrims and Seekers*, SPCK, 2006.

2 See Hannah Ritchie, *Not the End of the World*, as in Chapter 17, note 31.

3 For example, using renewable energy rather than fossil fuels is appreciated by many people now, whereas ten years ago it was a minority concern; there

are also more electric cars on European roads now than there were a decade ago; and recycling, vegetarianism, and other features of a more sustainable way of living are on the increase. These are simply indicators of changing attitudes. For an introduction to and synthesis of new economic thinking see Kate Raworth, *Doughnut Economics*, as in Chapter 17, note 32.

4 For example: Psalms 42, 44, 59, 63, 137, and the book of Lamentations.

5 See, for example, Neil Paynter, *The Sun Slowly Rises: Readings, Reflections and Prayers for Holy Week from the Iona Community*, Wild Goose Publications, 2017; Ruth Burgess & Chris Polhill, *Eggs and Ashes: Practical and Liturgical Resources for Lent and Holy Week*, Wild Goose Publications, 2004; and the renewed interest in the service of Tenebrae in many churches.

6 Brian McLaren's book, *Life after Doom: Wisdom and Courage for a World Falling Apart*, Hodder & Stoughton, 2024, takes the reader through this process of grief for a world that is being destroyed.

7 For a brief overview of the Christian Movement see Linda Woodhead, *A Very Short Introduction to Christianity*, Oxford University Press, 2014. For a comprehensive history of the Church try Diarmaid MacCulloch, *A History of Christianity: The First Three Thousand Years*, Penguin, 2010. For examples of Christians working for justice, peace and care for creation see christianaid.org.uk; cafod.org.uk; iona.org.uk; greenchristian.org.uk.

8 You can read the full version in 1 Kings 19.

9 See Chapter 11, note 15.

10 The Western Medieval Church had a bonus here in that it claimed that without its ministrations no one would go to heaven, thereby giving it enormous power and wealth. On Jesus' attitude to wealth see also Luke 12.13–21.

11 Kate Raworth, *Doughnut Economics: Seven Ways to Think Like a 21st-Century Economist*, Penguin, 2017. This model is based on the fact that we humans are a part of the life of the world, and its recommendation of working for human flourishing rather than the accumulation of wealth fits well with the values of the reign of God. Examples of earlier resettings of economics which align better than consumer capitalism with the values of the reign of God include E.F. Schumacher, *Small is Beautiful: Economics as if People Mattered*, Blond and Briggs, 1973; Erich Fromm, *To Have or to Be?* Jonathan Cape, 1973; and Margaret Legum, *It Doesn't Have to Be Like This*, Wild Goose Publications, 2002.

12 See Luke 22.25–27.

13 In *Life After Doom*, chapters 8 and 9, Brian McLaren advocates learning from indigenous peoples and sees parallels between the experience and wisdom of North American indigenous peoples and those of the writers of the Bible.

14 In 1968 the United Church of Canada published a new creed, an edited version of which was included in the *Iona Abbey Worship Book*, 1988 edition:

> We are not alone,
> we live in God's world.

We believe in God:
who has created and is creating,
who has come in Jesus,
    the Word made flesh,
    to reconcile and make new,
who works in us and others
    by the Spirit.
We trust in God.
We are called to be the Church:
to celebrate God's presence,
to live with respect in Creation,
to love and serve others,
to seek justice and resist evil,
to proclaim Jesus, crucified and risen,
    our judge and our hope.
In life, in death, in life beyond death,
    God is with us.
We are not alone.
Thanks be to God.